EYE TO
THE HILLS

EYE TO THE HILLS

A Scotsman's Memories of an Outdoor Life

Campbell Steven

breedon **books**
PUBLISHING

First published in Great Britain in 2001 by
The Breedon Books Publishing Company Limited
Breedon House, 3 The Parker Centre, Derby, DE21 4SZ.

Dedication
For my children Helen, John and Kenneth.
Also remembering with sincere gratitude all the many companions
on and off the various hills of a lifetime.

BY THE SAME AUTHOR:
The Island Hills
Scotland (Panorama–Books series)
The Central Highlands (Scottish Mountaineering Club District Guide Book)
Glens and Straths of Scotland
Enjoying Scotland (Foyle's Travel Book Club Choice)
The Story of Scotland's Hills
Proud Record – The Story of the Glasgow Fire Service
An Anthology of Hope
Enjoying Perthshire

ISBN 1 85983 272 5

Printed and bound by Butler & Tanner, Frome, Somerset
Jacket printing by GreenShires Ltd, Leicester

CONTENTS

Chapters 12, 13 and 14 first appeared in enjoying Scotland, Robert Hale and Company, 1971.

Chapter One

CLYDE-BUILT

HOISTED aloft at an upstairs window to see the *Aquitania* – four red funnels, black-topped, barely moving beyond an in-between scattering of trees. Such was the make-up of my earliest memory.

The big Cunarder – at that time the largest liner in the world, and later to become known as 'the ship beautiful' because of the grace and symmetry of her design – would have been on her way from John Brown's at Clydebank to her trials on the Clyde, thence to Liverpool and a maiden voyage to New York.

The date – some time in April 1914, the month of my third birthday.

It is only as I have been flicking through my tattered mental scrapbook of personal memories – old now and jumbled as a junkyard – that I have come to realise how important a part in the background of the early boyhood days was played by the Firth of Clyde. Our home was in Helensburgh, spread out along the northern shore, and day in day out as the seasons swung, we looked across the miles of the estuary to Port Glasgow and Greenock and Gourock, dark against the sun, and the low whale-back of Renfrewshire hills. A smoke-blurred line, they made a fit backing to a restless, never-ending to and fro of shipping: liners and freighters, dredgers and hoppers, lighters and puffers, tugs and paddlers, even every now and again during World War One grey armadas of warships and troopships.

A world almost unbelievably different from the tame, empty Firth of today. And all – so far as I was concerned at that time – taken completely for granted.

Accepting this as normal was due in part to our family life and in particular to our involvement in the world of engineering. For 65 years – the whole of his working life – my father shared in the ups and downs of the family lift manufacturing firm, A. & P. Steven, established in Glasgow by his father and uncle back in 1850. No doubt therefore, in the occasional 'business' talk at meal times round the family table, there would be enough news from the endless stir and bustle of the river to fire any youthful imagination.

Helensburgh itself had long held an honoured place in shipping history. It was the town's first provost, Henry Bell, who had masterminded the building of the world's original steam ship, the 30-ton *Comet*. Designed to sail 'by the power of air, wind and steam', the

Winter Invitation. On a ridge of Ben Vorlich, near the head of Loch Lomond, photographed by my daughter Helen.

little vessel made her down-river debut from the Broomielaw to Greenock in August 1812 'at a speed of five miles an hour against a head wind'. The achievement earned Henry Bell himself the title of 'father of steam navigation in Europe'.

To mark the *Comet*'s centenary her flywheel and the anvil which had been used in her construction were placed in Helensburgh's Hermitage Park. For me these became quite commonplace bits of scenery, when in due course I came to trail past them every day on my way to and from school.

Every now and again we would pay a family visit to Glasgow, more often than not to the dentist, and then we would glimpse from the train window as we passed Yorkhill and Queen's Dock, a jigsaw of wharves and tugs, of masts and cranes and ropes and funnels, blue and yellow, black and white and orange-red. In the earliest days, of course, we knew no names to match the colours. But what matter? The privilege was ours to be seeing a whole world that not so very many years later would virtually cease to exist.

Now and again during World War One days, when Britannia really did have a navy sizeable enough to rule the waves, the Home Fleet would move in on brief visits. Attended by their retinue of cruisers and destroyers, that majestic battleship quartet, *Queen Elizabeth*, *Warspite*, *Barham* and *Valiant*, would pass through the boom defence lower down the Firth and take station off the Tail of the Bank. For a day or two they would stay, then as unobtrusively as they had come, they would be gone.

Other clear memories are of the fine searchlight displays that were sometimes put on, no doubt after the Armistice. On one occasion, too, when the fleet was in, we were able to go aboard *Barham*, a wonderful thrill for a youngster. Not indeed that any precise recollections of gun turrets or range finders, torpedo tubes or searchlights are even vaguely with me today; what I do remember is being shown a superb scale model of *Barham* herself and on it a jagged scar made by a shell splinter – oddly enough in exactly the same place as the battleship had been hit and severely damaged in one of the Home Fleet's engagements not long before.

Nearly 30 years later, in November 1944, I was to see *Barham*'s sister ship *Warspite* again, this time in action pounding 15-inch shells into Westkapelle, on the Dutch island of Walcheren.

Two other World War One naval incidents – one humorous (in retrospect), the other tragic – remain with me. The first concerns Britain's – and the world's – second aircraft carrier, HMS *Argus*, nicknamed the 'Flat Iron' on account of the absence of any superstructure. It happened during her trials on the Clyde. Family pride was deeply involved through the fact that she was equipped with a special A. & P. Steven lift carrying the wheelhouse and bridge, which could be recessed during actual flying operations. Family pride, however, received a correspondingly big dent when it was learned later that

All dressed up for the baby parade.

the lift had got ignominiously stuck between decks, trapping – to the horror of all concerned – the inspecting admiral and his entourage.

The other incident, unforgettably tragic, was the loss of the submarine *K13* in the Gareloch, on 29 January 1917. Newly built at Fairfields in Govan, *K13* submerged for a test dive, but because four ventilator hatches had been left open, the boiler room was flooded and she was unable to resurface. Eighty sailors, civilian workers and Admiralty officials were on board; 50 miraculously escaped. Tragically, however, despite desperate rescue efforts, the remaining 30 were lost. On shore, watchers could hear the trapped men tapping on the sides of the sub, and I still recall the unbearable sadness we felt as we were told in school how the tappings were growing fainter, then finally how they had ceased altogether.

Also Clyde-built and up-front in a class of her own, HM battlecruiser *Hood* often used to lie off the Tail of the Bank. There could be no mistaking the formidable look of her and she soon became familiar as a local friend. All the blacker, then, for those who knew her, the day in May 1941 when the news was released that she had been sunk in the Denmark Strait by *Bismarck* and the latter's attendant cruiser *Prinz Eugen*.

Bulking much more largely in the background to those distant days – and indeed so commonplace as to be taken completely for granted – was the great coming and going of paddle-steamers up and down the Firth. In particular, 'our own' North British sextet became especially familiar. Based on Craigendoran, they could be seen from afar in the ample pier-space, no mistaking the red, white and black of their funnels: *Lucy Ashton* and *Dandie Dinmont*, *Kenilworth* and *Talisman*, *Marmion* and *Waverley*, each with special features which, in later years, made them easy to distinguish.

At around 5 o'clock in the afternoon, with the train commuters from Glasgow aboard, they used to set off from Craigendoran on their respective runs. The much-loved *Lucy Ashton* was best known to those of us in Helensburgh as her prerogative was always up the Gareloch, plus the crossing to Greenock and Gourock; the others made further down the Firth, to Kilcreggan, to Kirn and Dunoon and Innellan, and finally to Rothesay.

Now and again one or other of these runs would provide a special treat day for us. The chief delight, of course, was always to rush 'away down to see the engines', huge, gleaming, thunderous, smelling magically of hot oil. I can't honestly say I remember hearing anything of the notorious death-or-glory rivalry which went on between so many of the paddlers over the years, though it was always highly satisfactory, making for one of the piers down the Firth, to outstrip some rival – clearly inferior to whichever NB speedster we were aboard.

One somewhat unorthodox passenger to take a trip 'doon the watter' was the dachshund belonging to one of my Helensburgh aunts. Grandly named 'Kitchener' – and suffering sorely on account of this World War One patriotism when the local toughs, reckoning him to be German, used to pelt him with stones – he disappeared one day and

My parents in the garden of 'Edenkerry', where we lived in Helensburgh.

could not be found. He was eventually located in Rothesay and, having failed to get a return ticket when he set off, had duly to be retrieved, no doubt in a certain amount of disgrace.

Very conveniently we possessed a vague family relative who lived in Craigmore, just along the waterfront from Rothesay itself. Sometimes, though never often enough, we would stay for a day or two with this elderly courtesy aunt. From her windows we had wonderful viewings of an exciting new world – of the Caledonian Railway or Williamson boats with their yellow or white and black funnels; of the Glasgow and South-Western paddlers such as *Mercury* or *Jupiter*, even on occasion of that twin-funnelled pair, the palatial *Lord of the Isles* and her great rival, the world-renowned *Columba*. Brave days indeed!

Still more exciting for us as youngsters were the two big turbine steamers *King Edward* and *Queen Alexandra*. Sailing all the way down the Firth to Campbeltown, they used to be particularly popular with holidaymakers bound for the west side of Arran – Loch Ranza, Pirnmill (where passengers were ferried by small boat to and from the jetty) and Blackwaterfoot. Three summers running, on our way to Southend at the foot of the Mull, we were able to enjoy sailing on one or other turbine, our holiday adventures having begun when we crossed over to Gourock on the *Lucy Ashton* for the change to the Campbeltown boat.

Strangely enough, neither these holiday sorties far down the Firth nor our occasional visits to Rothesay ever seemed to bring us into any near contact with the world of yachting. Often, of course, we heard talk of the Clyde Fortnight, of keen racing for the Seawanhaka Cup, of visits by the royal six-metre *Britannia*, uniquely black-hulled. But the millionaires' province began at Hunter's Quay and we never happened to pass that way at the right time for spectating. It was still to be many years before the explosive dinghy takeover of every corner of the Clyde.

Three of our uncles – and to a much lesser degree our father – were in fact keen enough on sailing, though just how skilled they were I do not know. Now and again we would hear snippets of tales of rounding the Mull and facing into wild Atlantic seas, although I rather wonder if Crinan was not more often in favour. All this was really before my day and certainly in my experience we were only sketchily nautical as a family. The nearest approaches to seamanship that I can recall – and sadly they were rare enough – occurred when our parents would hire a rowing-boat and we would cross the mile of the Firth to Rosneath for a picnic. These voyages to another world were tremendous fun, although always without fail in the late afternoon the wind would swing round to the east and strengthen wickedly so that our parents would have to toil without let-up at the oars to get us back safely to the pier at Helensburgh.

Sometimes I wonder what their thoughts would have been had they been watching on the shore of the Gareloch some 80 or so years later as their granddaughter, on peace protest bent, paddled her kayak across the bows of the most recent Trident submarine inching menacingly through the Narrows at Rhu.

Autres temps…

Chapter Two

STARTERS

IT is difficult to think of a happier place to have grown up in than Helensburgh. That is – it has to be said – if you lived a fair distance up the hill. Down town at the time of World War One there were still plenty of bare-footed boys to be seen about on the cobbles. Not on the streets higher up.

Our house, 'Davaar', was situated just about the middle. Level with the town's Hermitage Park. And when, in 1915, we flitted eastwards to 'Edenkerry', in Havelock Street, the latitude was very much the same.

In those days, of course, the town was far smaller than it is today. Beyond us, for example, there was no Kirkmichael housing scheme, only the antiquated curling pond and Kirkmichael Farm flanking the Old Luss Road, past the muddy trickle of a burn where eels took our occasional worms rather more often than did trout. Those, too, were the days when every morning Caldwell, the Craigendoran dairy farmer, came round with his horse-drawn milk cart; and each dark evening, not long before our own candlelit bedtime, 'leerie' with his long flame-topped pole would be doing his round to light the gas of each street lamp in the town.

Our family in 'Davaar' consisted of my parents, my brother Douglas, six-and-a-half years my senior, and myself. My younger brother Colin was born in 1915 and it was then that we moved to the larger house, 'Edenkerry'.

Quite early on and very sadly Douglas developed severe asthma and this handicapped him miserably; indeed it was to blight the whole of his life. Soon after the outbreak of World War Two, in 1940, he died of pneumonia while attempting to play his part in the Local Defence Volunteers (later, of course, the Home Guard).

Especially during the damp winter months Douglas had to spend much time in bed. My mother was endlessly patient with him, heart-saddened to see him so ill and suffering so dreadfully, with only haphazard allergy diagnosis and little helpful treatment available. Constant nursing, much of it by night, taxed her own health severely and meant that domestic help in house and kitchen was essential.

Helensburgh in those days may certainly have been a mere skeleton of its ample size today, but we could still lay claim to a useful flock of relatives – one grandfather, two grannies, five aunts, an uncle, three cousins and one or two others more distantly perched on the branches of the family tree. This had its advantages, for example financially at Christmas and New Year, when – if fortune smiled – a visit might well produce a florin or half-crown. On the other hand, the less attractive side of the coin meant 'official' visits and on special occasions the misery of having to perform party pieces in front of an audience of aunts clearly determined to gloat over our discomfiture.

There were other, more distant, relatives who also looked in to see us now and again, among them a rather more elderly cousin who on one occasion met with dire misfortune in Glasgow. He was proceeding to unlock the door of his early model saloon car parked in Argyle Street underneath the Hielandman's Umbrella, and trying to remove one of his gloves with his teeth. Unfortunately he tugged rather too vigorously and his upper denture was projected into the path of an oncoming red tram, destination Dalmuir. The rest of the story is shrouded in discreet mystery.

Starting as it did in 1914, World War One came to be more or less accepted as an ongoing aspect of our everyday life. Talking about it, thinking about it and in due course reading about it meant that it was an ever-present reality throughout all its four years. Undoubtedly the most vivid memory of it that I retain is of the day during the Battle of the Somme when the telegram arrived to say that an uncle, a lieutenant in the Cameronians, had been killed in action. Later on, too, news came through of a first cousin reported missing; in due time presumed killed.

Regularly we pored over the pictures in *The Illustrated War News*; obediently answering the appeal of the Red Cross, we went out and gathered sphagnum moss for wound dressings; inevitably we gave patriotic names to our pets (our much-loved black cat was called 'Foch' after the French field-marshal); reports of zeppelins and bombs over London triggered frequent terrifying nightmares. Even cigarette cards, frenetically collected, were mostly patriotic: 'Allied Generals' – Haig, Pétain, Joffre, Allenby and the rest – or 'Military Motors', including, I remember, one card depicting tanks, first used on the Western Front in the autumn of 1916.

At one of the darkest periods of the war a company of the town's worthier veterans was mobilised – a forerunner as it were of Dad's Army. Led by Colonel Denny, head of the Dumbarton shipbuilding firm, they came to be known none too respectfully as 'Helensburgh's Last Hope'. One of their more notable exploits was when, led by the Colonel on a fine white charger, they marched to the local infirmary to dig trenches – and filled them in again on the next parade day. The only other aspect of their training which I can recall having heard about was rifle practice in the local drill hall. This too was of rather doubtful value to the war effort, as the main achievement seems to have been when the town's leading doctor, carried away with patriotic zeal, succeeded in shooting out one of the hall lights.

Clearly digging trenches was in more people's minds than just the veterans'. At one time my brother and a friend had a notion to see what they could do in our garden and dug an impressively deep trench with no obvious exit in one of the flowerbeds. They then inserted me into it to make sure walls and roof were trustworthy, at which point, fortunately, my mother happened to spot what was afoot and had me prised out to safety by the heels.

On the morning of Armistice Day in 1918 we were at school, and great beyond words was our jubilation at the eleventh hour on the eleventh day of the eleventh month. For me the day was made all the more memorable when a blimp, the *NS7*, happened to fly low overhead as I was walking home. It seemed to add in a very special way to the wonderful rejoicing of the day. Only weeks later we were to be watching the famous *R34*, built in Renfrewshire at Inchinnan, doing its trials prior to record breaking as the first airship to cross the Atlantic non-stop from east to west.

My schooldays had begun when I was five – at Miss Johnstone's, Colquhoun Villa. Prior to my debut, Miss Johnstone had been instructing the young of Helensburgh, including two of my uncles, for approximately 30 years. In my time the roll numbered 16. All except four were seated six-a-side down an impressively long table with two at one end and Miss J. at the other; another privileged two, having reached dizzy heights at the head of the school, sat apart at the exclusive 'wee table'.

We had emerged from the days of slates, but not of copy books, and such sentences as 'Music hath charms' or 'Silence is golden' had to be scrupulously copied out, to begin with in pencil, then with graduation to ink. Much emphasis was placed on the learning of our tables, while on Fridays, rather more pleasurably, Scottish history tales were read to us – the only flavour I ever had of that in all the years of my schooling in Scotland.

Miss Johnstone was a strong Christian, a devoted member of the Congregational Church. Quite naturally, therefore, our school week started on Monday on a Christian note with a hymn or a few verses of a metrical psalm, all 16 scholars clustered around the not particularly young harmonium. Every Monday, too, we had a Bible lesson, well told. All preparation beyond price for the later challenge of the Christian faith. For me at least Miss Johnstone's was a wonderfully happy school and I have nothing but immense gratitude for the four far-off years of excellent teaching I received.

In those days, it need hardly be said, there was no mistaking when it was Sunday. At 10.45am the bells of some half a dozen church steeples started ringing out together in glorious disharmony. There were the Old Parish, St Columba, Park, St Andrew's and the West Parish; indeed the Congregational Church and the episcopal St Michael and all Angels may well have been contributing their more muted best besides. Altogether it was a rare concert which enlivened our 12 minute walk to St Columba, sometimes adding a touch of panic to our pace if – as happened often enough – someone would pipe up 'The bells have stopped!'

Usually our path crossed that of the Piggott family – father and several attendant daughters – heading in the opposite direction and on the other side of the street, for the Roman Catholic chapel. Much later in the thirties, Stephen Piggott was to become Sir Stephen for his part in designing the *Queen Mary* at John Brown's, Clydebank, while one of the not unglamorous daughters (whom we often partnered at local dances) was to go west to marry Senator Kefauver in the US. Not that there was any fraternising on those Sunday mornings: we would pass each other like ships in the night with no full recognition signals passing between us.

St Columba was United Free, only becoming Church of Scotland at the time of the Union in 1929. My father was an elder for many years and as he was very sociable believed in one visit and no more to an evening when he was on the rounds of his pre-Communion visits (unlike so many feeble card-on-the-doorstep calls today). In those more leisurely days this allowed time for ample chatting over a cup of tea.

There was, of course, no television then and not even the wireless. Sunday papers still had only a faint fraction of the importance they have scooped up for themselves nowadays and my father was never at all happy about buying a copy. This presented considerable difficulty when there had been some important sporting event such as a rugby international the day before. Strangely, however, on such occasions there would be urgent business to be discussed after morning service with the church beadle, the latter having had no awkward qualms of conscience over an earlier visit to the local newsagent's.

At home on Sunday afternoons Bible lessons were very much a feature of life. Stories were read to us and it seemed quite natural to have to learn by heart the books of the Bible, the ten commandments, the beatitudes, or other outstanding passages. Along with what I learned at Miss Johnstone's, I was certainly afforded a grounding to stand me in excellent stead in later years.

During the winter and spring school terms, Tuesdays were occasions of special importance: they were the days of Miss Webster's dancing class. Mums and offspring would repair to the Pillar (or lesser) Town Hall, where the ten or so kilted rebels and their more genteel female counterparts would be bullied to heights of deftness and decorum which would have done credit to the lawns of Holyroodhouse.

Miss Webster herself, tall, willowy and elegant, ruled parents and pupils alike imperiously as a queen: eightsome and foursome, highland fling and sword dance, polka and waltz and lancers – all went with a never-to-be-forgotten sombre dignity. Boys sat along one side of the hall, girls opposite, with a range of critically doting mamas parked in strategic viewpoints round about. Before each dance we would have to cross the floor and request – with touching politeness – the hand of a partner.

Over the years I never made it to the gavotte, my outstanding claim to stardom having been the occasion when, with three other unfortunates, I had to perform the sailor's hornpipe in the centre of the expanse of Glasgow's St Andrew's Hall. This soul-searing misfortune befell me on one of the rare red-letter occasions when we were bidden to an afternoon get-together with the young of other schools from as far away as Kilmacolm. To the music of a charismatic German leader, Herr If, and his band, the dancing was performed before an admiring parental throng for all of a long Saturday afternoon.

My first teacher, Miss Johnstone, outside her school, Colquhoun Villa.

Fortunately there was another, rather brighter side to this picture. During the Christmas holidays there were almost always four or five dances, given either in spacious private houses or in the Pillar Hall, and at these the Miss Webster brigade came happily into their own. Tradition had it that we were conveyed party-wards in one of Waldie's ancient cabs – or, less respectfully, growlers – horse-drawn and smelling of fusty leather. Usually on arrival we would be handed programmes so that we could book up each item in advance with the partner of our choice. After the last dance there was much lingering till it was announced that our cab was at the door waiting to bear us homewards.

In their day these horse-drawn cabs, from Waldie's widely known stable, were a real institution. Much in demand by those living in Helensburgh's exalted upper reaches, they came most obviously into their own when the business trains arrived in the evening. Ranged in an impressive line inside the station precincts, they awaited the arrival from Glasgow Queen Street of the 4 o'clock, the 5.08 or – for those really ill-used at the office – the 6.05. It was an impressive sight to see familiar business types being disgorged from their first-class carriages, half-flourishing their 'seasons' at the barriers and making for their favourite chariots.

Another Helensburgh custom was for one of Waldie's ageing growlers to be hired for

Bicycle parade. My mother, second from the right.

a picnic in Glen Fruin – a real highlight of the summer holidays. After the horse's long, wearied plod up the Luss Road, we would be joyously disgorged at the farm track just past the usual turn-off to the glen to make our way down to an ideal pool, sufficiently deep for a few yards of swimming, but not so deep as to be dangerous. Often we would have our cousins with us and then, as well as the usual burn-side ploys, we would have wading races, ending inevitably when disaster struck and someone fell in.

Apart from the Fruin, good places for bathing were few and far between. Helensburgh had no pool and the waters of the Clyde were not noted for their purity. Shandon Hydro (later burnt down), with its salt water indoor pool, offered the best opportunity, and when I was older there were some memorable visits to it from school. But Shandon was five miles away – far enough by bike in the holidays – and the cost, two shillings a time, was virtually prohibitive.

It seems almost as though there was a reluctance to depart from the custom of using the cabs, a slowness for cars to take over; or maybe to begin with the Helensburgh hill was less of a test even for the old nags. Cars were, of course, coming well into their own by the start of World War One, though our doctor, who was an early owner, still reportedly considered it advisable to sound his horn every time he was approaching a corner. For quite a few years, too, the first Dunbartonshire numbered car, SN 1, was to be seen in and around the town.

STARTERS

In those halcyon days the chief form of transport apart from Waldie's cabs was the bicycle. As a family we had early made our marks in cycling history: had not my father ridden his penny-farthing all the nine miles from Salen to climb Ben More in Mull? Back in 1894 had not my mother and two others caught the attention of a local reporter: 'In the cool of last evening I was taking a stroll along the road to Row (nowadays Rhu) at Helensburgh, when suddenly three damsels, pretty damsels, dressed alike in riding habits and mounted on safety bicycles, came tearing down a slight declivity. They raced smoothly together with their little number fives elevated off the pedals, their cheeks flushed, and their hair flying. Some distance behind came the grey-bearded pater on a pneumatic. I have seen ladies affect bicycling ere this, but my path has not yet been crossed with such a pretty turn-out. Now then young men, don't all wire at once for digs in Helensburgh, and don't sit out on the fences along the Row road, or I'll give no more hints.'

For us times have certainly changed, though I can still picture an elderly Helensburgh neighbour of ours who was so addicted to two-wheeled travel that even on rainy days she was to be seen out, pedalling nonchalantly along with her umbrella held aloft like a half-filled spinnaker.

One special craze of early days centred on the West Highland Railway, that outstanding scenic section of the old North British which became the LNER, which became British Rail, which became Scotrail, which became…

What really started me on the fanatical collection of names and numbers of the 4-4-0 'Glen' engines was the sight of *Glen Beasdale* steaming through Spean Bridge station one autumn afternoon in either 1916 or 1917. We were on a family holiday in Gairlochy and on this particular day my mother and I, having no doubt been in Fort William, were waiting on Spean Bridge platform for the Fort Augustus branch line train to take us the two miles back to Gairlochy.

The Fort Augustus line – so sadly closed not so very long afterwards – was, of course, single track and I remember how, with all the local men away at the Front, the lady of the house where we were staying in Gairlochy was acting as stationmaster, porter and signalman all at once. Passenger and goods traffic would hardly have been excessive, but her duties were certainly responsible, including manning the signal box and operating the single line staff system of those days.

But to revert to my 'Glen' engine craze… The line, which climbs in a wide curve from Craigendoran to Helensburgh Upper, passed just a field away above our Havelock Street house. It was simple therefore to nip over our back wall and race up the field in a couple of minutes for regular engine-spotting. No.153 *Glen Fruin*, 221 *Glen Orchy*, 100 *Glen Dochart*, 258 *Glen Roy* and so on… they became as familiar as the palms of my hands and are in no way forgotten 80 and more years on. Always there were new names to hope for; more often than not there was disappointment when, perhaps, it was only *Glen Fruin* or *Glen Douglas* over again.

Sometimes on our visits to Glasgow there would be 'Scott' class engines to be seen at Queen Street (Upper) and I have never been able to discover the difference between these 4-4-0 locomotives and the 'Glens'. Yet I saw only one of them on the West Highland line – *Dirk Hatteraick* heading a polytechnic excursion; on the other hand at Queen Street there would be *Meg Merrilees, Peter Poundtext, Dominie Sampson*, or some other Scott 'character'. Occasionally, too, there would be named 'Atlantics', the first of these, I remember, being *The Lord Provost*. But, exciting as all of these were, they were strangers to the West Highland. There it was the 'Glens' which reigned supreme and if at some future time of folly the ever-present threat of closure is realised, at least the wonderful old familiar 4-4-0s will never be forgotten.

Hardly with quite the same glamour as named locomotives, but none the less setting off almost as many bells of memory, were the adverts gracing the walls and stairs of Queen Street station. Mazzawattee Tea; Iron Jelloids; the Bovril posters – 'A Little Bovril Keeps the Doctor Away', 'Prevents that Sinking Feeling'; or that classic jingle:

> They come as a Boon and a Blessing to Men,
> The Pickwick, the Owl and the Waverley Pen.

Of the more strictly medical posters I have no recollection at all – as well, maybe, though not indeed that any of those unpopular remedies of yester year, Gregory's Mixture, Cascara Sagrada, or even castor oil, could ever have gone far toward popular acclaim.

Between Helensburgh and Glasgow there were always plenty of amusements both summer and winter. Most often during the Glasgow Fair Fortnight there were pierrot performances in the bandstand on the Helensburgh sea-front, while at the pier itself there were swimming galas, complete always with hilarious greasy pole antics. Occasionally in the big field at Craigendoran there would be a Bostock and Wombwell circus, or – better still – a Wild West Show. I well remember a real 'Red Indian' coming to our gate at 'Davaar', shaking me by the hand and inviting us to one of the evening shows.

Nor did any Christmas holidays seem complete without a visit to Glasgow and Hengler's circus, with its unforgettable Wild West climax – canoe after canoe shooting the rapids of a real waterfall into a real pool on stage.

In the days of Charlie Chaplin and the silent film, Helensburgh could boast two cinemas, La Scala and the Cine House. The latter was perhaps more renowned for its insect population than for the quality of its films and I well remember my one and only visit after I had pestered my mother till she gave way to my badgering and accompanied me to see *The Four Horsemen of the Apocalypse* – a singularly uncomfortable non-success.

Undoubtedly the greatest influence on my early life, apart from that of my parents, came from my brother Douglas. He was born in 1904, six-and-a-half years before me and, as mentioned before, was sadly handicapped by ill-health. Seeing me always fit and well must often have added to his distress, yet never once did he say so. Even in later years he made no mention, leaving me now a life-time later feeling guilty that I was not more understanding, far more sympathetic.

To help Douglas, especially during his worst attacks of asthma, my mother regularly read aloud to him. And naturally I was often a not unwilling eavesdropper. Some of the books were far beyond me, even if at times I would pick up snatches of their drama or their humour. But boys' books, for example G.A. Henty, or Percy F. Westerman with his war stories, were real meat and drink, and I remember well one or two fat bound volumes of the *Boy's Own Paper* – happy and gripping alternatives to my own weekly absorption in *Rainbow*. Douglas himself was an avid reader, making up for his sketchy attendance at school with a range of knowledge that was almost unbelievably wide.

One of the various hobbies at which Douglas excelled was working with wireless equipment. In the early days, of course, this had to do with crystal sets. He learned how to make these (how, I know not) on drilled ebonite panels with crystal and cat's whisker, condenser and – before the days of loud-speakers – headphones. I would watch and fumble away at making my own, thus inevitably learning a great deal about how to interpret circuits and so on in books and magazines. The only broadcasting station we could receive was Glasgow (5SC) 23 miles away, although I remember being convinced that I had managed to hear Manchester. London (2LO) was too far distant; it came later when we progressed to valve sets. These were mostly two-valve, for which Douglas would find circuit details in the various wireless magazines. The expert in those days was Scott-Taggart and we would try out his suggested combinations with varying success; ST100, I remember, was especially good. It was altogether an intriguing world, and I am truly grateful for the knowledge I gained of accumulators, high-tension batteries, rheostats and the like.

Another indoor ploy at which I tailed along with happy incompetence was small-scale woodwork. While Douglas produced fretwork presents immaculately finished – picture frames, mirrors, jigsaws – I would potter clumsily amid broken saw blades in a wasteland of glue. It was much the same with model warships made from wood and cork and pins, copied faithfully from *Jane's Fighting Ships*, scale 50 feet to one inch. We built up our own fleet, learning as we went the details of a World War One naval picture never forgotten. As often as not the models would be sold in the family market-place, to long-suffering parents or indulgent aunts (destroyers sixpence, cruisers a shilling, battleships half-a-crown).

Despite his severe health handicap, Douglas still managed to enjoy a remarkable variety of outdoor pursuits. For one thing he was no mean golfer, for another he later became a keen motorcyclist, even going over to the Isle of Man on at least one occasion to help in the pit of one of the riders in the TT.

In the early days, however, it was in natural history that he excelled for me. His bird-nesting skill was remarkable; indeed how he managed to find some obscure nests when nowadays I have to confess I find it hard enough just to spot the birds themselves, I simply do not know. Nor was his interest restricted to birds. On his wall he had a chart of animal tracks; on his bookshelves authors like Ernest Thompson Seton, G.D. Roberts and H. Mortimer Batten spoke for themselves.

One other ploy which has continued down the years to give me immense pleasure has been interest in butterflies. In the past, of course, butterflies were far more numerous and widespread than they are today, so it was not difficult for us to build up quite a useful collection, especially as somehow Douglas learned how to set and mount and above all to distinguish species, sex and so on. Helensburgh's fields and moors were good for all the various ordinary kinds; for the blues we relied on holiday habitats on the East Coast.

Strangely enough one kind we never saw was the orange-tip. Yet nowadays in Perthshire gardens in May these are relatively common. Often I think how elated my brother would have been to add one more to his not unimpressive list.

*****

When I was nine I moved up to Larchfield Academy, a stone's throw across the street from Miss Johnstone's. During the war Larchfield had been a secondary school and it was there that John Logie Baird had been a pupil. When I arrived on the scene it had shrunk to prep school status; as that, however, it was thriving, and for the most part it did me proud over a happy four-year span.

The standard of work was high without being too demanding, but it was the emphasis on every kind of outdoor activity, organised and disorganised, which made those years so memorable.

Cycling – once I had learned to ride – played a major and certainly unorthodox part. It tended to be of the dash and crash variety, especially as in the family we never seemed to own a new machine. Extra gears were too sophisticated, and for riding after dark, if we bothered about lighting up at all, we had oil lamps (needing endless cleaning) and later on acetylene. Much later still dynamos took over, though to our way of thinking, they were the prerogative of the ultra-rich and far beyond our reach.

So far as dash was concerned, two-and-a-half minutes to school might have qualified, while there was more of crash in the bicycle polo tussles which we sometimes engaged in on our front lawn.

One devastating ride was after golf one morning of the holidays. Three of us – my brother Colin, the local dentist's son and I – decided to make our homeward way all on one bike, a machine of uncertain vintage and more than dubious braking efficiency belonging to our friend's mother. We reached the unsurfaced, cindery foot of the steep hill below the golf clubhouse at impressive speed, but there, unfortunately, there was a sharp bend to negotiate. We finished in unorthodox fashion – in a heap. Those were the days when the remedy for all doubtful wounds was liberal application of iodine, and for a week or two we had to suffer the torture of regular anointing while piece by piece grit was removed from knees, hands and elbows.

In our mild West Coast winters really lasting snowfalls happened all too rarely, and we

Picture from the past. My brothers, Colin (left), Douglas (centre) and myself.

had to make the most of such arctic days as we did have, usually with sledges in the steep field below the golf course. At first we had to make do with an ancient family toboggan which looked as though it had seen service with the Flintstones; later we graduated to a more sophisticated 'Flexible Flyer'. The steep streets of the town, of course, seemed purpose-built for sledging. However, variations of the sport there were officially frowned upon, possibly following the apocryphal incident when an intrepid sledger in full flight down the Luss road had to pass between the legs of a horse pulling a cab across one of the major crossroads.

Another aspect of winter sport in Helensburgh was skating. According to a minute of the Town Council dated 1 October 1870, an agitation for a skating pond in the town was resolved by 'an offer from Sir James Colquhoun to grant a piece of land adjacent to the lower reservoir for a skating pond under the control of the Magistrates and Council.' The popularity of this new amenity was never in doubt (in its earlier years it was also used as a summertime pond for model yachts) and many a winter's day was enjoyed on it by experts and novices alike.

Skates were of many strange sorts and shapes, mostly screwed on with more optimism than effectiveness and all equally liable to fall off. Ice hockey games were open to all and sundry with fire in their bellies, provided some sort of metal was fixed to the soles of their boots. Nobody had any idea how games began; never, certainly, how they ended. Suddenly they would flare up, then just as quickly die down, only to burst into fast, furious life once again. Walking sticks or even tree branches were brought into murderous play, though I cannot remember if we ever had any kind of puck. Speed and aggression were all that mattered.

In summer things were more orderly and sedate. Cricket held leisurely sway except on the first Saturday of June when the school sports took place – a very special occasion with a marquee and the Helensburgh pipe band in full regalia. I think we were too sophisticated to have an egg-and-spoon event, but there were three-legged and sack races, with clock golf for the more sporting parents and a tug-of-war for the band. All in all a day to remember.

It was in 1920, when I was nine, that I had my first game of rugby – and was hooked for life. In course of time this led to inclusion in the school team and the first match – a dour 3–3 tussle with a Glasgow Academy fifteen on the main New Anniesland pitch, somewhat flatter and vaster than the lumps and bumps of Larchfield.

Each autumn my father used to bring home the small pocket guides produced by the well-known outfitters Forsyth's and Rowan's, with the club fixture lists, the rules and, most fascinating of all, a record of all the Scottish internationalists and their 'caps'. Mondays would see me with the day's paper, assiduously copying into the Rowan's guide every club result from the previous Saturday.

One very special reward for being in the school team was to be taken each December to New Anniesland to see the inter-city match between Glasgow and Edinburgh. To be able to watch heroes such as Dan Drysdale, Eric Liddell, J.C. Dykes or Johnnie Bannerman was bliss beyond telling, a first big step toward interest in the international scene.

A bonus in hero worship came our way, I suppose in 1922 or 1923, when Eric Liddell stayed with us for a weekend during a student mission to Helensburgh. This meant that at the 1924 Olympics we took a more than mildly proprietorial interest in his historic triumph.

The following January – as I was by then at school in Edinburgh – my father took me to see Scotland defeat France in the last international to be played at Inverleith. Then, two months later, it was to the opening match at Murrayfield, that heart-stopping see-saw win over England which appropriately gave Scotland the Triple Crown, the Calcutta Cup and the championship.

The early Murrayfield internationals saw the usual ups and downs in Scottish fortunes. But for me at least they were classic games fought out by legendary players: the famous all-Oxford three-quarter line, on the wing Ian Smith, mighty of pace and stride; the start of the Nelson-Waddell partnership at half-back; forwards rousing stand and terracing to the great rallying cry of those days, 'Feet, Scotland, feet!'.

Regrettably my own rugby career carved no notable niche for itself in history. Carefree days at Larchfield came to an abrupt end when in my last match I was removed from the scene of action with a dislocated elbow. At school in Edinburgh I played scrum-half with little chance of getting the better of my opposite number, W.R Logan, who was later capped 20 times for Scotland in the early thirties. Finally, in only my second college game at university, a broken arm suggested calling it a day. Only interest remained undimmed.

Chapter Three

GOLF

IT MUST have been, I think, in 1934 that I decided to give up competitive golf. There comes a time when anyone who reaches the stage of doing little but play golf, think golf, talk golf, even dream golf, becomes an intolerable bore. Such a time had come for me and there was only the one thing to do about it. Strange maybe but true, in the 65 and more years since then I have never had any least shreds of regret.

It was fairly late on in World War One that I actually started playing. Precisely where, I have no recollection, though as our parents were keen, if mostly holiday, players, it probably happened on some remote country course where rabbits were not out of place.

My first club was a cleek, a horrible weapon like an old-time putter with a fraction of loft. It had, I remember, a black grip, slippery as seaweed, and it stung with every mis-hit shot like a badly sprung cricket bat. After a year or two, the acquisition of a mashie was a landmark never to be forgotten. Those were, of course, the days of hickory shafts and non-rustless heads, so that after every round there routinely had to be much polishing with emery paper and brasso.

This was rather later than the feather ball era, but it was necessary all the same to decide between playing 'floaters' or 'non-floaters', the latter, being heavier, supposedly more manageable on windy days. When I started, balls were not recessed or even 'dimpled', but had 'raised' covers like brambles. When, some years later, recessing did come in, I remember one very special ball I possessed, a 'Patent Colonel'. It had crescent-shaped dimples, with a red crescent at each end, and was my pride and joy. Alas, I think it was stolen; it disappeared after a perfectly good drive and was never seen again despite a prolonged search. A suspicious-looking character had been lurking in the deep hollow where my drive had ended up and doubtless made off with a useful potential repaint. I nearly wept over the loss.

From the cleek and mashie era I graduated in due course to a brassie and my performances were upgraded accordingly. This led to holiday membership of our home course in Helensburgh, undoubtedly possessing some of the most beautiful views in all Scotland. From the high fifth green, carved out of an old pine wood, one looked across moors to a part of Loch Lomond and its islands; in the opposite direction far down the Firth of Clyde and over the Renfrewshire hills to 'the Sleeping Warrior', the ridge of the high tops of Arran. I cannot remember exactly how testing the course was in those earliest days,

Golf, with Douglas, at Helensburgh.

except for the tribulations of the short 17th, then a road hole, and the 'Mirror of the Moor' at the short third, a small peaty pool surrounded by birch trees and heather, which had a fatal magnetism for wayward shots and trapped many more balls than ours.

The Helensburgh club professional, Tom Turnbull, was there for many years and was always a good friend to youngsters who sometimes got scant consideration from tiresome old stagers, horribly akin to P.G. Wodehouse's 'wrecking crew'. Even the most funereal four-ball would refuse to let us through when we could have raced twice round the course to their once. Tom was also a good club-maker, and today, 75 and more years on, I still have one of his clubs, a hickory-shafted mashie-niblick, which serves me nobly on the rare occasions when I do sally forth.

As the years rolled on, we came to know every blade of grass on the Helensburgh course. Improvements made to its layout and quality were accepted, usually without serious question, just as our own scoring dropped and wavered and dropped again. There was, however, one major drawback to our progress – a lack of opportunities to play over better, more testing, courses. Inevitably rounds elsewhere were confined to summer holidays, immensely pleasurable but of no great teaching value.

One course of much delight was Kingussie, on Speyside, looking over to the western ramparts of the Cairngorms. Its winding hazard, the Gynack burn, was one ingredient of the fun, although by contrast in the very early days I had found the long second hole more of a heartbreak; I remember struggling to achieve a 19 there on both of my first two rounds.

Three successive summer holidays were spent at Southend, near the Mull of Kintyre.

In those distant days (I have no idea of its make-up today) it was sandy and sun-blest and very special, with a fiery-eyed bull named Geordie frequently at large in the rough, and innumerable rabbit holes to trap even quite reasonable shots. I well remember once marking the hole down which my ball had disappeared and bringing up two other balls from its depths before I retrieved my own.

At home I was especially fortunate in almost always having one or both of my brothers as opponents. Later on my younger brother Colin was to win the Helensburgh club championship and to play for Glasgow University. My older brother Douglas, greatly handicapped by ill-health, had fewer opportunities than either Colin or myself. He was none the less a very adequate performer and we had not a few excellent 'away' games, notably on both the Old and the New courses at St Andrews. Another memorable occasion was the morning at Prestwick, when Douglas managed to put his drive at the first hole beside the railway through the adjacent signal box window.

Boarding-school days in Edinburgh brought better opportunities to gain experience. For example, for the summer terms we were allowed to have our clubs and also our bicycles, so that on 'off' days we could escape up to the Braids for a round. Better still, by invitations on special occasions, we enjoyed a game on Mortonhall with one or other of the masters.

Well remembered, too, are summer holidays with school friends, just as keen as I was, who lived near East Lothian courses such as Gullane 1, 2 and 3, Longniddry, or Kilspindie, all excellent for experience.

Unless memory plays tricks, those were the days when peg tees were coming into use, replacing time-honoured sand. By no means all irons were rustless. The 'Schenectady', or centre-shafted putter, an innovation favoured by some, was well and truly banned. Trolleys, it need hardly be said, were unheard of.

My schooldays ended in 1929 and in the autumn of that year I went up to Oxford. My tussle with Modern Languages, at Queen's, was meant to last three years, but two mishaps upset the timetable completely. A broken arm at rugby was an unpleasant interlude in my second term, and – much more serious – a bad motorbike smash at Easter the following year, resulting in a compound fracture of my left leg, a cracked wrist and a nearly severed nose, caused even more havoc. With time for convalescence and extra spells in Germany and France, I ended up with an overall span of ten terms in actual residence.

With rugby and football both out of the window, golf came, almost unnoticed, into favour. I knew Southfield, the Oxford course, from occasional rounds in early days, but I had not taken it particularly seriously. However, at the end of my summer of convalescence, we had had a family holiday at Lossiemouth, and several tentative rounds there – especially some needle four-ball matches with my brothers and the Lossie pro, George Smith – had whipped up renewed enthusiasm. Now, with some honest application, the chance to enter a new, excitingly competitive world seemed there for the taking.

GOLF

The Southfield course, with its heavy, muddy fairways and hard slogs at some of the long holes, was anything but generally popular. Its rival, Frilford Heath, found much more favour with some, but as it was several miles away, its appeal was only to those who had transport. My own growing familiarity with Southfield became a kind of love-hate relationship, for although the disadvantages were frustrating enough, there were undoubtedly several holes of character to make amends. The monthly medals, too, were always enjoyable challenges, and with several successes in these, I managed eventually to get my handicap down from four to two.

Another course, even more distant than Frilford, was Huntercombe, and one day in November 1930 I was invited to play there in a friendly four-ball. Before my game had had a chance to go to pieces, I was fortunate enough to get a one at the 165-yard second hole. Also by chance, after our round, Sir William Morris (later Lord Nuffield) who actually owned the course, happened to be in the clubhouse and willingly signed my card – ever since a much-treasured memento.

It was always a special pleasure to watch the top players of the Varsity team in action. There were usually one or two Americans in the side and I still remember clearly the glimpses I had of Bob Baugh, from the States, who was captain in 1929–30 and who played off plus four. He was, I consider, one of the two finest swingers of a club I have ever actually seen in action. (The other was the all-time great Joyce Wethered, later Lady Heathcoat-Amery, whom we watched playing over Lossiemouth in 1931).

Two other Americans who were 'up' during my time were the Sweeny brothers, Charles and Robert, who was later to go on to win the British Amateur in 1937. They acquired the reputation of never being beaten at Oxford as a foursomes partnership, but this was not so – E.L. (Ted) Dunnett and I accounted for them on our way to winning the scratch foursomes competition (the St Andrews Cross) at Southfield. I think they must have been a bit below their best that day and I remember Charles on the ninth tee observing drily as Bob's drive soared far off course, 'Gee, Baaby, you sure swayed like a ship at sea'.

Ted Dunnett, who was a great friend at Queen's, played twice in the Varsity match against Cambridge. He was a relentless opponent, maddeningly steady, and I had more successes against him on the putting green – where we played regularly for a twopenny Cadbury's flake per hole – than actually out on the course. His home was in Sussex and we had some great holiday battles on some of the fine courses there he knew so well.

During my spells of swotting abroad I was first in Germany and then in France. Rather optimistically I carted my clubs around with me. Continental golf in those days was different from what it is today: courses were few and very far between and players tended to be considered as wealthy as they were eccentric. For the Wannsee course in Potsdam, where I was staying, I managed to scrape together the necessary green fees and had a game or two: one with the British pro there for the price of his fee (thus doubtless costing me doubly dear), another with a Herr Mendelssohn-Bartholdy, who was somewhere in line of succession to the great composer himself and I imagine a better golfer.

My stay in Paris later on was different. There were no opportunities for ordinary, run-of-the-mill outings, but I happened to discover that the French Open was due to be played at Saint Cloud, in Paris, the only course I had ever heard of in France apart from the equally glamorous and exclusive Le Touquet. As those competing were to have the privilege of two free practice days before the event itself, this seemed to present an opportunity I couldn't miss; things looked in fact like taking a turn, however brief, for the better.

My entry was accepted, apparently without demur, and I duly enjoyed my two days of free golf. The only serious mistake I made was that on the first day I opted for lunch in the clubhouse; on the second – by then poorer and wiser – I snatched a few furtive mouthfuls of sandwich under the least conspicuous tree I could find. The event itself was duly won by A.J. Lacey, a mighty hitter of those days. I can't think that he was particularly worried by the opposition I put up: in the opening round I went out in a nervous 40, then tragedy really struck and inexplicably I had a 10. My 84 and an almost equally bleak afternoon round saw the end of an unimpressive career in France.

Back once again in more familiar surroundings, I tackled my final year of golf and study – too often, I fear, in that order of priority. So far as the golf was concerned, there were the usual start of term trials, with numerous contenders, old and new, teeing up for recognition. Among these there were four from Queen's, so we had a useful team ready-made for the inter-college cup, which in fact we did duly succeed in winning without any very great difficulty.

Invitations to play in the actual Varsity team meant wonderful opportunities to savour the pleasures of a number of famous courses. Two of these club matches in particular I remember well. The first was against Addington, where in the Saturday morning foursomes my partner and I halved with our opponents, one of whom was an illustrious London surgeon, Sir Harold Gillies. In the afternoon singles I again encountered Sir Harold. It was a close-run thing for 16 holes, by which time I had nosed ahead to dormy two. The counter-attack was bitter and looked like winning back the 17th – until I laid an impossibly dead stymie. The match-winning halved hole which resulted could hardly have been described as popular.

The other special memory I have is of my singles match at Worplesdon. I was drawn against the well-known cricketer B.J.T. Bosanquet, who invented googly bowling and who played off scratch. He was not at all a considerate opponent: he did five holes in an indecent 12 strokes, including a one at the 158-yard fourth. Needless to say, the match did not go as far as the 18th green.

As the weeks went by, my great hope was that playing in these club games would lead to inclusion in the team to meet Cambridge at the end of March and thus to a Blue. One by one the places in the Oxford side were filled until just two remained. My hopes were hanging on, if not altogether undimmed.

Austin seven Johnnie Walker *and its part owner.*

And, sadly, it was not to be.

I was invited to play in a Sunday match against Tadmarton Heath. That might well have been no different from any other club encounter but for one thing – the fact that Jimmy Moss, the captain, paired me in the foursomes with his Number Two, the secretary Cecil Middleton. I hardly knew Cecil and had never before met him on the battlefield either as partner or opponent. He was an impressive player, rather dauntingly inscrutable, and as he had clearly been briefed by Jimmy to take strict note of my performance, I felt anything but at ease. And I played like a hypnotised rabbit. Cecil, not surprisingly, was not exactly impressed. That, in short, was that.

The debacle, as I have said, was on a Sunday. And often enough since then I have wondered – who knows? – had I had the courage of Eric Liddell, things might have turned out differently. For me, if not for Oxford. Even without me they won the Varsity match comfortably.

That summer, after the horror of our final exams, Ted Dunnett and I enjoyed a memorable week in Scotland. In Oxford we had gone half shares in an ageing Austin Seven which cost us £26 and which, as it was still going strong, we duly named *Johnnie Walker*. In second gear it reached a respectable 41mph; in top, two miles an hour faster, perfectly adequate speeds for taking us north to my home in Helensburgh, the base for our planned campaign.

The June weather was faultless and our golf – by our standards – good enough to satisfy. In those distant days the St Andrews courses were not over-crowded and the Old Course gave us of its best. On Western Gailes, that tough Ayrshire test, we had the privilege and pleasure of a round with the late Sam McKinlay, who not long before had played in the Walker Cup. And we had a great tussle over the King's Course at Gleneagles – particularly well remembered on two counts. First of these was that for once I had the beating of Ted, only to be denied that when he sank an immense putt on the 18th green to square the match. The other reason was rather different: we had heard that the celebrated Hollywood actress Norma Shearer was to be staying at Gleneagles Hotel, so we decided to spend our all on afternoon tea there in order to see her and sigh from afar. We had tea indeed, but alas! there was so much feminine glamour arrayed about the lounge that we had to confess that we had no idea where or which was Norma. Great indeed was the frustration!

Next day in *Johnnie Walker* Ted headed south to Sussex, where he disposed of our faithful friend for the £26 we had paid in the first place. At least we recouped the cost of that afternoon tea.

In a way, for me, waving Ted off on his journey was symbolical. Although many years later, on a family visit down south, I did have another game with him over West Sussex, it was no more than a pale shadow, a poor goodbye to the days that were past. And although shortly after the Scottish tour I did play in one or two competitions, they were no more than half-hearted affairs, now barely remembered at all.

But then, as some sage once remarked, enough is as good as a feast.

Chapter Four

BIRDS

LOOKING back now over the years to our early Helensburgh days, regrettably a sad confession has to be made. A major outdoor obsession at that time was collecting birds' eggs.

Blame it, of course, on my brother Douglas. Quite inexplicably, in view of his constant ill-health, he was amazingly good at finding nests. My own skill never came anywhere near to matching his, only my enthusiasm as I tailed inexpertly along.

Blame – yes, indeed. But for me there is also the other, very different, side to the coin: the basic practical knowledge of birds which I gained. This was a bright thread which was to run through a lifetime of outdoor enjoyment, for me and indirectly also for my family. For it I can never be grateful enough.

During the Helensburgh schooldays we had endless opportunities, especially in the late afternoons and the lengthening light evenings of April and May. And such knowledge as we did not acquire within our own local ken, we gleaned from our ornithological bible of those days, Richard Kearton's seductively illustrated British Birds' Nests. He carried us off on plenty of fanciful flights to find scores of hopelessly rare nests, almost all far from the surroundings of the Firth of Clyde.

Yet, however glamorous it was for us as boys, I don't suppose our collecting was really very outstanding. In those days we had no car, and the distant limit of our territory was only two or three miles away at the old Black Bridge in Glen Fruin. Nearer home, of course, we were thoroughly familiar with the woods, the various burns, all the rough farmland and also the moors alongside Helensburgh's three reservoirs. Thinking of the moors in particular, I can still picture Douglas, ensconced in a tree at the edge with a telescope which had been passed on to him by a sea captain uncle, directing me to a curlew's nest we had found hard to pinpoint; on another occasion to a meadow pipit's with a very special prize in it – a cuckoo's egg.

One bird we never even thought of as being uncommon was the corncrake. Every spring a pair used to nest in the hayfield just behind our house – not that we ever saw one of the birds, so far as I can recall, and we certainly never found a nest. All we had to do was endure the craking night after night, night after wakeful night. Now the old field has grown a rich crop of bungalows and blackbirds; the corncrakes, I know, held sway at least until 1931.

The egg-collecting had come to an end long before the thirties. Yet, oddly enough, the bird-watching which took its place was little in evidence for a number of years, indeed until well on in the war, when I was in Cornwall.

The CO of our unit in St Ives, Major Geoffrey Rees Jones, was a keen bird-watcher and occasionally, after a day on the cliffs, I would sneak off with him and perhaps one or two others, to note what bird life was to be seen on the mudflats at Hayle, three miles away. The estuary there never lacked for interest and it provided me with two life-list additions – black-tailed godwit and spoonbill, the latter solitary, intriguing and unmistakable as it scythed tirelessly in the mud.

Another notable 'first' for me during the Cornish days was the green woodpecker, heard and seen surprisingly often in the woods near St Ives. Yet my most remarkable wartime memory is not of any life-list sighting but of a song.

It was in Germany just before the crossing of the Rhine. I had spent the night in a shell crater watching wave after wave of RAF heavy bombers obliterating the town of Wesel on the far side of the river – a thunderous, flaming inferno, the nearest approach to hell I have ever seen. With dawn came silence. Then, quite near me, as the light gradually increased, a skylark took off. It climbed with an outpouring of song so beautiful, so wonderful, that for several minutes the night's ghastliness was forgotten; briefly I seemed to be glimpsing heaven.

After the war, life in Glasgow had much in it of difficulty and stress; and as the fifties slipped into the sixties, there came the added tribulation of deep family sadness. It was not an easy time.

Then, as the clouds parted afresh, there were new beginnings. One entailed a move back to Helensburgh – a strangely different place to me after an absence in Glasgow of a quarter of a century, yet with a whole world of details to recall days that were past. Ten years' residence there were followed by six in Crieff and, in 1982, by yet another move – over the hill to Aberfeldy.

In that second Helensburgh era there were one or two incidents most certainly not be forgotten. One was the irruption into our garden by way of the garage roof of half a dozen waxwings. Very considerately they proceeded to settle for a bite to eat on the cotoneaster immediately below our sitting room window, so that we had a prolonged view of their jaunty crests and 'sealing wax' scarlet from a range of two feet.

More distant were two sightings I had of the bird I called 'stranger on the shore'. One day I was travelling by train to Glasgow, and passing the mudflats between Dumbarton and Bowling, spotted what I was quite certain was a flamingo. Not surprisingly my report of this was greeted with ribald disbelief. Indeed it was all voted such a huge joke that I almost decided my glimpse must have been no more than a pattern of dirt on the railway carriage window – only it so happened that the next day at exactly the same time, in exactly the same place, I saw the bird again. That really made it necessary for us to go *en famille* and investigate. Duly then, we were approaching the mudflats when another pair of walkers

Sitting gannets crowd the ledges and top of 544ft Stac Lee, St Kilda.

came toward us and, surprisingly, stopped to speak. 'Excuse us,' they said, 'but we're a couple of reporters from a Sunday paper and we've been sent to check on a story that a flamingo has been seen hereabouts lately. We don't suppose by any chance you've seen it?'

Needless to say, birds of prey have always been of special interest, even if our actual record of sightings has not been particularly impressive. A red kite in Perthshire and a hobby in Inverness-shire have possibly been our most outstanding; on the other hand, merlins and hen-harriers have been disappointingly rare. Ospreys nowadays are quite obliging both at and away from their 'sheltered housing', while golden eagles can seem almost like old friends in Perthshire and the Islands.

One predator we seem to be especially feeble at recording is the sparrowhawk, yet on one occasion I was very nearly taken as an authority on it. A fellow scribe of mine during much of my 40 years of contributing to *Scottish Field* was the outstanding natural history writer, the late David Stephen. With similar sounding names it was inevitable that he and I were occasionally mixed up with each other. One day I answered our phone to be asked by the caller if he was speaking to Mr Stephen. All unsuspecting, I assured him that indeed he was.

'Well,' came the voice, 'will you please tell us what we should do with a baby sparrowhawk which we have here in the bath?'

Up on the moors above Aberfeldy, beside the high road to Crieff, we can often watch short-eared owls. Our best viewing was one May morning when we were taking a young enthusiast, Duncan Boyle, on his first real bird-watching outing. Immediately opposite Scotston farm a short-ear kindly allowed us all of four minutes' viewing at ten yards range, as he sat nonchalantly on a fence-post. It was a good start to Duncan's day, and only a field away some blackcock were strutting the last few minutes of their morning lek. Then, not too long afterwards, we were repeatedly whinnied at by a short-tempered osprey not far from its nest.

Always of interest on each year's bird calendar are the familiar 'firsts' – the February oystercatchers, speedsters back from the coast, screaming in follow-my-leader to their patch down beside the river; late in April the first uncertain willow warbler refrain in the wild garden birch trees just round the corner; the excited greetings of the swifts in early May; the first skein of autumn greylags just in from the Iceland lava-fields, never too tired for garrulous talk-back.

My most memorable encounter with our wintering geese was on the saltings of Wigtown Bay early one December morning in 1964. Local wildfowler, the late Robert McGuffie, was my guide and mentor, taking me in pre-dawn blackness over half-seen fences and zigzag ditches to partial concealment in a narrow, muddy creek. Waiting there we could faintly make out the excited talk of the geese further out by the tide's edge; congregated in their hundreds, they were calling and clamouring, impatient for the time to fly inland to their grazing. Then, as the darkness lessened, the greylags began taking off, at first sensed rather than seen, to settle only yards from our hide-out. Shortly after, they were followed by the pinkfeet, swinging in like bombers in a fly-past to add to the knots and clusters all round us. It was a truly remarkable sight, hundreds of geese grazing contentedly only yards away. Sadly, however, as the light increased and monochrome gave way to colour, it became only a matter of time before we were discovered. Noticeably uneasiness spread; a few coveys took wing and melted away. Soon, without fuss or panic, the whole company had taken off. Finally, I remember, as Robert and I got stiffly to our feet to look around, the saltings were empty.

Holidays nowadays take us almost invariably north or west to the Islands, rarely abroad, and on the few occasions that we have been away from Scotland, birds seem to have played a remarkably small part in the scheme of things. I do remember, many years ago on the Mediterranean fringe of the Pyrenees, the completely silent, rather spooky 'buzzing' attacks by large Alpine swifts, but of other birds I recall none; on that particular holiday the varieties of superbly exotic butterflies were more memorable attractions. Much more recently, when camping in Norway, we saw a pair of bluethroats on the lower scrub slope of Brurskardknappen, a gentle Scandinavian 'Munro' of 4,796 feet, which we were about to climb. Elsewhere in Norway we were surprised at the number of magpies we seemed to see everywhere, also the many fieldfares and redwings. It was amusing to think how we might be meeting some of the latter again in the autumn when we were back home in Perthshire.

Seabirds, with almost no part at all in land-locked Perthshire, are enjoyed all the more on holidays or special red-letter days of island-going: fulmars and eiders, kittiwakes and tysties; Manx shearwaters when visiting Colonsay or the Garvellochs; always in the north the occasional skua; the prodigal scattering of auks and puffins on the sail past the Old Man of Hoy.

Terns I like to think of as belonging especially to the islands of the Forth. Still well remembered is a visit to Fidra and a picnic lunch where we had the accompaniment of an incredible bedlam of screeching, screaming terns. These we casually took to be all common or arctic. Then unexpectedly in the middle of all the din one of our party, an authority on the Forth island birdlife, pricked up his ears and remarked: 'Did you hear that? A roseate.' We were duly impressed.

One real seabird regret is never to have been out to the relatively small Scar Rocks gannetry in Luce Bay, or far north to those of Sula Sgeir and Sule Stack. However, there has been good compensation in almost touching a few gannets on the crowded Bass Rock shelves and peering down the 400ft Ashydoo face on Ailsa Craig to wonder at its great thousands-strong concourse of nesting birds. St Kilda, too, has had its memorable moments – sailing through a snow-swirl of gannets off Boreray, or craning one's neck to see the whitened zigzags of sitting birds on the incredible rampart of Stac Lee.

The lack of a real coastline is indeed Perthshire's one big drawback from the bird-watcher's point of view. The brief stretch of the Tay estuary at Invergowrie is simply not good enough. It is a restriction, however, which has lent interest to the rules of a childish game which we have been playing each May now for quite a number of years. This is simply a contest to see a hundred different kinds of birds in the month – no serious problem for the 'all-or-nothing' fanatic, but for ordinary mortals with day-to-day business to attend to an altogether sporting exercise. To begin with we allowed ourselves the whole of Scotland as playground, then to make the game more interestingly difficult, we restricted the boundaries to Perthshire, thus immediately with the 'no seabirds' handicap.

Over the years our 'century in May' has given us enjoyment limited only by the quick passing of the month. There are never enough days to allow us to fit in visits we fancy, from quartering the high tops near Drumochter for dotterel or ptarmigan to checking for magpies on the look-out for cast-off jewelry near the Gleneagles dustbins. On the other hand, there are many places where we know to look for old friends – 'stonechat corner' for one; for another, one of the loch territories of the black-throated divers. Precise timing, too, can be a useful help: for example, by knowing within approximately two-minute parameters of their deadline just when the woodcock start roding in the gloaming at the foot of Drummond Hill.

Population changes can sometimes mean pluses or minuses on the month's list. For instance, the whooper swans which brought up a family of four on little Loch an Daimh, below the northern flank of Schiehallion, sadly decided the following year to set up home elsewhere. On the other hand, golden plovers, not always easily located up on the moors, chose in 1996 to feed for several days and remain at night in a low-level field near Bridge of Gaur, congregated in a flock numbering more than 40. There is always so much of variety, so much of interest.

As each May came and went and we reached much the same total, I suppose we reckoned we must be doing rather well; short of making it all into a full-time job, we had got as far as we could. Perthshire, it seemed, really hadn't a great deal more to offer.

That is, until the autumn of 1997, when we met Robin Hull.

Not long retired from his most recent post as Professor of General Practice at Amsterdam University, Robin – half a Scot – and his wife Gillian had the excellent good sense to come and live at Strathtay in the heart of Highland Perthshire. Engaging with most welcome enthusiasm in local community activities, the Hulls were quickly very much part of nearby Aberfeldy life.

Having taught – and watched birds – in every continent, including Antarctica; having been high in the Andes, and even, in the Garhwal Himalaya, having followed the course of the Rishi Ganga river into the sanctuary of Nanda Devi above what has been described as 'one of the most terrific gorges in the world', Robin had collected a world bird list numbering more than 2,000. Yet not for a moment did such immense bird-watching experience stop him from getting down to finding out what Perthshire had to offer.

Out and about, he gave us directions as to where we could see shovelers and black-necked grebes, a pair of ruddy duck and nesting red-throated divers. We were even given a map reference to help us to see a pair of pied flycatchers. Indeed it might almost have seemed as if we were not quite as proficient as we had imagined.

On one bright March morning Robin and Gillian whisked Mais and me away on an outing to Montrose Basin, excellent Tayside territory familiar to them, though only once briefly visited by us in the distant misty past. Our hopes for the day were high.

With the car parked at Bridge of Dun, we followed along the meanderings of the South Esk till it finally widened and lost itself in the expanse of the basin. It was very much a stop-go walk, as Robin had his telescope with him and Mais and I were more than happy to pause and benefit admiringly from the way nothing escaped his notice – not even a twite perched with its back toward us on a hawthorn bush above the far bank of the river.

On the river itself a trio of remarkably unconcerned dabchicks made a good introduction to the flotillas further on – mostly goldeneye, teal and wigeon. Redshanks and peewits were busy on the mud-fringes, while half-hidden by the banks in front of them, pinkfoot sentinels kept periscope watch on our progress. With a whole raft of eiders out on the basin itself, the morning's tally could certainly be said to have given us a more than ordinary appetite for Gillian's picnic lunch.

Perthshire bird watch. Another for the list?

Part two of the day was a visit to the Scottish Wildlife Trust's observation centre, perched suitably high for far viewing out over the basin. By the time we arrived there the tide was full, so that the birds were mostly crowded on the mud-spits and islets. At long range it was not too easy to make accurate sightings, although it seemed too much like cheating to keep consulting the closed-circuit TV monitors for confirmation. Of most interest perhaps among all the oystercatchers and dunlin and purple sandpipers were the two or three bar-tailed godwits; surprising in a different way the half dozen moorhens attracted to the food scraps scattered right under our noses just below the hide itself.

With the addition of an obliging two or three on the way home, the species count – admittedly thanks in part to Robin's quick eye and sure-fire diagnoses – climbed to a truly satisfying height. All in all a day to remember.

Chapter Five

NEW HEIGHTS

S O far as I can recall, our parents in their day had no great tales to tell of exploits on the Highland hills, much as they loved them. My mother did occasionally relate how she, with some friends and family, had gone astray on Goatfell and been benighted. It was all very uncomfortable, but at least – in those more robust days before mobile phones and Sea King rescues – they made their own way down after daybreak in time to stop the search party from Brodick from getting properly under way.

My father, in addition to his penny-farthing expedition to climb Ben More, Mull, had been up Ben Nevis. This was in the days of the telegraph office at the summit and he used sometimes to tell us of the telegram – more thrifty than imaginative – which he sent from there to one of his sisters: 'Cup tea top Ben Nevis.'

However, these days apart – and just possibly Ben Lomond and Ben Cruachan also excepted – I cannot recall having heard tell of any other high level outings.

So far as my own tale is concerned, as for so many others it was the Cairngorms which had me hooked fairly and squarely with their lures. First it was Braeriach one brilliant August day in 1927 – a long, hot walk in to the old first bothy, then up to the plateau by the delightful eastern arm crooked round Coire an Lochain. We lunched at the summit and I remember well how immensely impressed I was when our leader, seeing a wisp of mist drifting in from the west, announced that he was taking a bearing on the Einich Cairn to keep us on course for our descent down Coire Dhondail. It was all a magic introduction to the high tops, long years before Munros became the common currency of the Highland hills.

The descriptions in Seton Gordon's classic, *The Cairngorm Hills of Scotland*, published by Cassell in 1925, fairly put the imagination into top gear, and I was fortunate enough to be able to do Cairn Gorm itself and Bynack More that same first year. For the former, of course, there was no mechanical uplift in those days; one had to foot it all the way from Glenmore Lodge to the summit and a ritual drink at the nearby Marquis Well – for us that day even icier than the rain beating into our faces and down our necks.

Third of those three August milestones was a 24-miler from Glenmore Lodge over Bynack and down to the Shelter Stone and back, memorable mainly for the seemingly endless contouring of the wickedly rough slopes of Cairn Gorm's Coire Raibert dropping down to Loch Avon.

These three were appetite-whetting outings, just the right mix for a beginner's starters:

sun and sweat on Braeriach; battering of rain on Cairn Gorm; a satisfying toil of miles over Bynack. All a foretaste of the pattern to come.

Not surprisingly, as we were enjoying a Speyside holiday again the following summer, August 1928, we made for the high tops when chances offered. Ben Macdhui was an obvious first choice, only disappointing in the event, when rain harried us relentlessly to the top over the long bleak desert above the Lurcher's Crag.

Unknown to us at the time, it was only three years previously, in 1925, that Professor Norman Collie had disclosed the details, familiar enough now, of his earlier uncanny encounter with the Big Grey Man: how, on his own and in thick mist, he had been pursued by sinister footsteps as he ran scared all the way down from the summit to the more rational levels of the Lairig.

For our part, with no un-diagnosed spectre breathing down our necks, our own descent beside the March Burn was rather less precipitate.

With two more outings that second August – to Beinn Mheadhoin and again to Braeriach, this time by way of the Sgoran Dubh–Sgor Gaoith round above Loch Einich – we were well and truly captivated. Indeed it was virtually a whole new world that had been opened up to us, not just that of the Cairngorms themselves but of the Scottish hills in their entirety. Wide new horizons stretched ahead.

To begin with opportunities were limited. We had no car of our own and transport to the hills more often than not had to be by train or bus. Living as we did in Helensburgh, it was to Arrochar and Crianlarich that we started to go most often. North of Tyndrum – had we been able to get as far – it was the time when the old Glencoe road, not much better than a cart track, had been replaced – not without some strong opposition – by the highway we take for granted today.

Not surprisingly The Cobbler and Beinn Narnain feature largely in the records and as the summers and winters went by, they were indeed to receive a remarkable variety of visits from friends and family far and near. The Cobbler in particular always has its own special attractions, not least of course the actual summit rock. The natural window through which one ordinarily crawls never fails to intrigue newcomers. In the distant past it was known as 'Argyle's Eyeglass' and tradition had it that to prove his worth every chief of the Clan Campbell had to climb through it to the top of the rock. In 1972, in pursuit of facts for an article I was writing, I wrote to the then Duke of Argyll to ask if he was familiar with the legend and had in fact been on top of the rock himself. In a very kind reply he said he knew of no tradition associated with The Cobbler, but that back in the twenties he had indeed done the climb as he wanted to compare the view with that from the top of his own local Munro near Inveraray, Beinn Buidhe.

In the earliest thirties our activities were not wholly without setbacks. For one thing university exams were deliberately timed to coincide with the only decent weather of the summer. For another I was temporarily inconvenienced by a compound fracture of the left

First Munro. The summit of Braeriach, second highest of the Cairngorms.

leg (and it has to be admitted that this also made golf rather more difficult too). Enthusiasm, however, was only temporarily curbed and we were soon out and about again.

In those early climbing days equipment for my brother Colin and myself might fairly have been described as basic. Raincoats with the skirts chopped off made useful anoraks; ice-axes were at least second hand; our boots were quite simply tackety. With the last, however, we clearly had to do better and in due course we made our way to Peter Dickson, in Glasgow's Hope Street, to be shod with impressive clinker-nailed heavyweights. Our sense of importance knew no bounds when we were advised to go off and break them in somewhere 'in an easy chimney.'

As the thirties went on, clinkers gave way to tricounis – on boots by then acquired from Robert Lawrie. The latter's London shop in Bryanston Street, near Marble Arch, was a real Mecca, and if we happened to be in the south, it was always a pleasure to drop in and discuss weighty mountain matters over a welcome cup of tea. Later of course, by the war's end, tricounis in turn were well on the way out and the reign of vibrams had begun – excellent indeed if of reputable make, quite simply lethal if merely pseudo and cheap.

It hardly needs to be added that pre-war our 100ft rope was Arthur Beale's best, garnished with its red strand of excellence. Karabiners, nuts, bolts, ice-screws and the rest were unheard of; the hammering in of a piton was generally considered too unsporting to be mentioned.

Early in the thirties Colin and I had joined the Junior Mountaineering Club of Scotland, which required no entry qualifications, and we had soon come under the influence of kindred enthusiasts. Like not a few others before and since, we learned much by trial and error – more often, it has to be admitted, by error than by trial. Rain, hail, shine or snow, the more we discovered the more we quite simply felt we had to know at first hand. A prospect to relish.

*****

In the summer of 1933 two grants of £10 each from the Everest Foundation enabled a college friend, Geoff Harker, and me to go climbing in Skye for a fortnight. Before the interviews which we had to undergo I had not been optimistic: Geoff, who came from Appleby, had no previous climbing experience, his knowledge of Skye was barely discernible and in his enthusiasm he could so far forget himself as to talk eagerly about the 'Quillins'. However, he must have conjured up sufficient charm to influence the committee's decision. They granted our request and we were all set to go.

In 1933 the journey from Helensburgh to Glen Brittle was a challenge. Admittedly the 'new' road through Glencoe had been completed – just. But there were three ferries to contend with: Ballachulish, where invariably the question was 'Would we be quicker going round by Kinlochleven?'; Dornie, where I have a diary record of one wait (southbound) of four-and-a-half hours; and Kyle, after breakneck jockeying for better placing in the queue all the way from Dornie. Finally there was the miserable road on Skye itself, with the eight-mile Drynoch–Glen Brittle climax, a stream-bed threat to every unsuspecting sump. In all, usually, it was a temper-testing trial of some eight to ten hours.

We travelled in Geoff's ageing Morris Minor, stuffed so full, I remember, with camping gear and food that two or three mealy puddings which my mother had added to our stores kept sliding about all over the floor. It was late afternoon when we reached journey's end, the sky scoured clear of cloud, the weather seemingly set fair. Happily we humped our mountain of gear to a pleasant little knoll looking seawards down Loch Brittle. Then we pitched the tent, cooked our evening meal and settled down to enjoy the aura of a golden sunset. A sense of well-being reigned supreme.

NEW HEIGHTS

Next morning rain was streaming down from a bleak, leaden sky. It had been so wet that when we knelt on all fours to unfasten the tent door and have a look around, the water level reached above our wrists. The island was already intending to live up to its reputation after all. As Sheriff Nicolson aptly put it:

> If you are a delicate man,
>> And of wetting your skin are shy,
> I'd have you know, before you go,
>> You had better not think of Skye.

It was not long before we met up with kindred spirits in the glen. Michael Peacock was a South African, a Rhodes scholar at Oxford and a rugby Blue. He was staying for six weeks in Mary Campbell's thatched but and ben. I imagined he was also studying, so there was no great difficulty in enticing him into going with us to 'the Ridge'. Michael was one of the most humorous characters I have ever met; not surprisingly he became a barrister and was much in demand as an after-dinner speaker. Tragically, just seven years later, he was to lose his life as a fighter pilot in the Battle of Britain.

Geoff and I wasted no time in moving from our knoll with a view to a more sheltered spot near Glenbrittle House. The rain, however, was determined not to let up and consequently we were more than happy to accept an offer from Mr MacRae to let us move into his spacious barn. Nor indeed was it only the rain that we were escaping. The walls of our tent, seemingly impregnated with some particularly succulent substance, had been much to the liking of the local cattle-beasts. Even worse, all the midges on the West Coast of Scotland had discovered that we could provide what may perhaps be most accurately described as a 'movable feast'. They were certainly as greedy as those of the Gareloch, where, in the picturesque idiom of Para Handy, 'ye'll see the old ones leadin' roond the young ones, learnin' them the proper grips.'

In the barn things were better, apart that is from the welcoming earwigs. Happily these tended to be less aggressive than the midges, and any invaders which ventured to approach single-handed were easily repelled, more often than not from the depths of our sleeping-bags with our tent-peg mallet.

Another visitor to the glen, Charlie Hatch, had come up by motorbike from Southport at apparently lethal speed in order to enjoy a brief hit and run encounter with Cuillin gabbro. He too had lost the battle with rain and midges and, in moist disarray, was only too glad to join the refugees. His climbing experience was clearly below par, not so his enthusiasm and we were much impressed by his footwear – a pair of Robert Lawrie's tricouni-nailed shoes. An expedition with him and Michael looked to be a worthwhile start to our programme.

Unfortunately there was no sign of the weather relenting and a damp and rather aimless morning ended up with a decision to try to cross the Thearlaich-Dubh gap – that superb breach in the main Cuillin Ridge into which, according to our guide book, 'It is recommended that a party of tourists should not all descend at one time, in case they might have to remain there permanently.' This choice was a mistake on our part. If there is anywhere in Britain, or in all Europe for that matter, more cheerless than the Thearlaich-Dubh gap on a day of dank mist and icy, driving rain, imagination fails to reach that far. Undaunted nevertheless, we made our way up to the Ridge and the gap, where our Lancastrian friend volunteered to descend the vertical short side. With rapidly freezing fingers we uncoiled the rope, tied him on and proceeded to peer anxiously after him as he disappeared into the murk. For some minutes all seemed to be going reasonably well. The rope paid out all right, if with rather ominous slowness, then suddenly through our unskilled hands with an even more ominous rapidity. However, as this was followed at once by a commentary of almost breath-taking pungency from the impenetrable depths of the mist, we concluded that a landing of sorts had been made and that no actual fatality had occurred. In due course, by a series of manoeuvres not yet described in any of the rock-climbing manuals, our friend was hoisted from his place of peril, after which we retreated valleywards in very damp disarray.

An action day at the far end of the Ridge seemed clearly called for, so after a typically leisurely breakfast, Geoff, Michael and I drove round to Sligachan. The tops were actually clear as we were setting out, but it was a promise made to be broken; scowling clouds were soon drifting in and rain started bouncing down on the moorland pools. We had a thoroughly enjoyable climb nonetheless – Sgurr nan Gillean by the Pinnacle Ridge – then set about the descent by the West Ridge. In 1933 the great feature of the latter was the bulky gendarme blocking the way. According to the original SMC *Guide Book*: 'This is a fearsome-looking place, narrow and shattered, with a great boulder planted on the ridge and blocking the way. Such is the grim aspect of the spot that one is not surprised to learn that the climbers who first described this part of the ridge "smoked a pipe over it" before they ventured to make the passage. When the pipe was finished, they crossed it without difficulty.'

Our own experiences were not particularly awesome either then or when we paid return visits in later years. Sadly the old policeman is no more. Having been on traffic duty since the pioneers first traversed the Ridge, he fell from grace in a big way during the winter of 1986–7. Great indeed must have been the fall thereof.

We had been only briefly in residence in the barn when we were joined by a well-known Midlands mountaineer of those days named H.V. Hughes. His moving in was not exactly a major operation; he was the most expert lightweight camper I have ever met, seeming almost to be able to stow away his belongings, tent and all, in his pockets. In addition to this he was a born entertainer and his lively rendering of the *One Fish Ball* song was the star number of more than one hilarious evening in the barn.

Looking across Coire Lagan, Skye, to Sgurr Dearg and its highest point, the Inaccessible Pinnacle.

EYE TO THE HILLS

For Geoff and me the addition of Hughes to the party was in fact no ordinary bonus; he influenced the whole pattern of the rest of our stay. For a start he willingly shepherded us up the Window Buttress on Sgurr Dearg, a good gymnastic warm-up for any day. From there we went on up the Ridge to the Inaccessible Pinnacle, a great grey dinosaur crouching in the mist. We were duly impressed, but even in the rain the pinnacle's short side, with its awkward mantelpiece tilt at half-height, gave remarkably little trouble. Hughes thereafter went nonchalantly off on his own down the longer east side, copiously furnished with holds, but nevertheless that day a greasy knife-edge seemingly suspended over nothingness. The remaining three of us followed at a more sober pace.

The weather after this actually cheered up a little, allowing us to discover further new parts of the Ridge, cross over to Loch Coruisk and, inevitably, visit the Cioch. Then came perhaps the best day of all, when Hughes led us up Collie's Climb on Sgurr Alasdair – an airy delight high above Coire Lagan, with the climax our first time on a Skye summit free of mist.

For a final treat he took Geoff and me to sample Slanting Gully on Sgurr a'Mhadaidh, assuring us that it was a thoroughly enjoyable climb. So indeed it was – for 150 feet. At that point a chunk of gabbro the size of a cricket ball came adrift at my handling and – despite my shouted warning – landed unkindly on Geoff's forehead. The climb, of course, was abandoned despite Geoff's protests that we should carry on; indeed he was clearly not feeling, and certainly not looking, particularly good as we helped him across the moor to the road. Later, however, attended to by a Drynoch doctor deft at stitching and fortified by a masterly Hughes dinner in the barn, he seemed to be restored more or less to normal.

This was virtually the end piece of our stay and although it was an unfortunate climax, it did not really mar the satisfaction we felt as we looked back over the fortnight. Our achievements had been negligible and the rain had been wet, yet it had been a good introduction to the ups and downs of the Ridge, perhaps for sheer enjoyment as rich as any among the succession of Glen Brittle holidays we were to have over the next few years.

Year after year we returned so that no summer seemed complete without a visit. Occasionally we renewed acquaintance with the barn. Once or twice we stayed at the post office, enjoying with immense appetites the homely fare which in those days Mrs Chisholm never failed to put before us. We even endured occasional nights of camping.

Holidays all the same had a way of being almost impossibly brief. One well-remembered July we had dashed north to see how much could be crowded into a single week, when, to make matters worse, a telegram arrived midway through summoning me to a job interview near London. Fortunately those were the days of the air service linking Glen Brittle with Renfrew, and a plane was due that afternoon. Duly surviving the humps and bumps of the 'airstrip' take-off, the de Havilland Moth took me comfortably on the first lap; I caught the *Night Scot* south, had a good interview, returned again overnight and ended on the bus to Sligachan. There my brother Colin and Sandy and George Spence, of

Dundee, were waiting like a sheriff's posse to hustle me off across the moor to the Bhasteir Tooth, that jagged black fang bared defiantly against all comers. Our route was Naismith's – as agreeable an afternoon programme as one could have wished – and my companions had already been out in the morning doing the Cioch Direct climb almost at the other end of the Ridge. Those were the days!

In September of the following year we went back to pay another visit to the Tooth. This time, in contrast to the airiness of Naismith's, we chose the route through the innards of the old fang, a dark cavern with gutters and gables and a narrow burrow exit high in the roof. This was the North Chimney route, climbed initially in 1906 by L.G. Shadbolt and A.C. MacLaren, who later were to be the first to do the traverse of the whole Cuillin Ridge in a day.

The only awkward part of Shadbolt's climb is a move from a steeply sloping shelf up on to the actual floor of the cave, and in the lead I was finding this more than a little puzzling. As I huffed and puffed and fumbled, I became aware of a couple down on the screes below watching me with more than passing interest. Then the man started calling up directions, in particular describing exactly the key to the pitch – an obscure handhold high up on the left wall. I took the advice, got up the pitch and turned to shout thanks to our helper. But the pair had gone. Later we learned who they were – Mr L.G. Shadbolt and his wife.

Our days at the north end of the Ridge always ended in the same way, with a sumptuous evening meal at the Sligachan Hotel. On one occasion there we had the pleasure of meeting another mountaineering 'giant' of the past, Norman Collie. Unfortunately, owing to his deafness, we had no great conversation with him; it would have been good indeed to hear at first hand perhaps of how he had 'discovered' the Cioch back in 1906 or to listen to a tale or two of days with his old companion and friend, John MacKenzie, whom he had trained and accompanied on so many classic exploits. As it was, we found it sad to observe him sitting all evening by himself, not easily approached, seemingly very much alone with his thoughts.

Standing on its own well away from the sweeping sickle of the Ridge is the fine twin-topped peak of Blà Bheinn, or more familiarly Blaven (3,045ft). The traverse of its lesser neighbour Clach Glas (2,590ft) along with Blaven itself makes a first rate scramble, and in July 1935 we had it in mind to do it if the chance occurred. It did, unexpectedly, when some boatmen from Soay who had been visiting Loch Brittle offered to take us round to Loch Scavaig on their way home. From a base camp somewhere near Camasunary we reckoned this would allow for a real day to remember.

Most memorable, in fact, was the almost unbelievable beauty of our evening view of the Cuillin. The sky was cloudless, the sun some time down as we made quietly up to the head of Loch Scavaig. Ahead, the sunset background was vivid beyond description, from azure overhead through green and lemon and gold to a furnace of flame. And against these colours, starkly chiselled in every detail of edge and kink and corner, the whole line of the Ridge, jet black beyond the great unseen hollow of Coruisk.

Unfortunately our peace was not to stay unbroken. As we landed we were met, not altogether hospitably, by two estate men. We could not camp there, they informed us; we must go two or three miles up the glen, beyond the march fence. As it was getting late and we still had to find a camp site, pitch the tent and cook our supper, we could not help feeling that a kindlier welcome would not have gone amiss. However the walk would at least take us on our way toward the foot of Blaven, and the summer gloaming still had long enough to go. In the event all went well, not just our camp, but the next day's climb and, in due course, the hike back to Sligachan.

The gruff welcome at our landing point had an amusing sequel. In March 1940 I was in Chamonix with the 5th Scots Guards and one evening at a café meal I happened to sit next to a fellow guardsman who told me he was from Skye. Rambling on in reminiscent vein, I chanced to mention Blaven and the frosty Loch Scavaig reception we had had. 'In fact,' I added, 'the one man in Skye I'd quite like to confront is the owner of that estate!'

'That's interesting,' my companion commented. 'He's my father… and when this war's over, how about coming across and visiting us? I'll be happy to fix up a day's stalking for you.'

All in all those pre-war holidays in Skye were unforgettable; they and the various good friends we shared them with are certainly unforgotten. We performed no outstanding feats. But the climbs we did do, from Sligachan, on Sgurr a'Mhadaidh and Sgurr a'Ghreadaidh, visiting and re-visiting above Coire Lagan from the Inaccessible round to Sgumain, the Dubhs and the rim over-topping Coir' a'Ghrunnda – rain, hail and shine we came to know them more than ordinarily well.

If one outing had to be chosen as most enjoyable of all, it would, I think, have to be the day of unbroken sunshine in July 1935 when Iain Jack, Colin and I idled across the Girdle Traverse of Sron na Ciche, up and down and along to fill eight hours of supreme contentment.

So enthusiastic were we, that on the final day of one holiday, when we were facing the long drive home, we got up really early before we left in order to visit the Cioch one final time. I remember this particularly well, as, while waiting my turn on the screes, I managed to fall asleep.

*****

In 1934 the scrutinising committee of the Scottish Mountaineering Club – in benevolent mood maybe, but of course with excellent good sense – approved my application for membership. Times, it should be added, were different. Fair qualifications were needed indeed: good, sound familiarity over several years with the Scottish hills, summer and winter, with rock and snow climbing experience to match. But always then the emphasis was on all-round competence and genuine love of the hills, rather than on any quickly acquired gymnastic expertise.

Ben Lawers

At 3984 feet, **Ben Lawers** is the highest mountain in the southern part of the Scottish Highlands. It lies to the north side of Loch Tay, and is the highest point of a long ridge that includes seven Munros. Ben Lawers was long thought to be over 4,000 feet , however in 1870's accurate measurement showed it to be some 17 feet short, prompting a group of locals to build a large cairn in the hope of bringing the summit above the "magic" figure. The cairn is no longer there, and in any case the Ordnance Survey ignored it, being an artificial structure.

The Ben Lawers National Nature Reserve encompasses nine mountains within the southern slopes of the Ben Lawers and Tarmachan Ranges, seven of which are Munros. It's a hugely significant place for botanists, being renowned for its rare and endangered species of arctic-alpine flora. The area is also home to a variety of wildlife including red deer, ptarmigan, black grouse and ravens.

This is a fairly easy climb as far as Munros are concerned as we start from a car park at just over 1300 feet (OSR: NN608377). This is reached by taking a minor road (signposted) off the A827 Aberfeldy to Killin road, about five miles north east of Killin. The route also takes us over Beinn Ghlas (3618ft), so we bag two for the price of one.

Exit the car park, cross the road and follow the trail which gently climbs through a fenced area which protects the ground cover from sheep.

Continue towards the foot of Ben Lawers' southern ridge. Keep right at the first path junction after which the climbing begins in earnest. The path, generally excellent, climbs easily in zigzags with no problems at all. As height is gained the view south across Loch Tay is superb.

The next section is steeper, but you soon reach the summit of Beinn Ghlas from where the route ahead is in view. Away to your left are some crags and an equally spectacular view north towards Glen Lyon. There is a descent here to a col before a steeper ascent up Ben Lawers itself. The path is excellent and the climb hardly noticeable as you head upwards to the summit, where you'll be rewarded with magnificent views of Ben Lomond and Glencoe to the west, and the Cairngorms to the north.

The simplest return is by reversing the route, or you can turn right at the col, and follow the path across the northwestern flank of Beinn Ghlas that will return you to the fenced off area and back to the car park.

As with all hill climbs, try to pick a clear day, as low cloud will obliterate your view.

Remember the safety precautions and the equipment required for mountain walks are as essential here as on the more isolated ones - weather conditions can change quickly, so check the forecast before you leave, take good care and always be well prepared.

Willie

My brother Colin enjoys the view over Glencoe from the west end of the Aonach Eagach ridge.

Today, by comparison, standards are almost unbelievably high. Snow and ice climbing in particular, with sophisticated techniques and achievements bordering on the incredible, has introduced a completely new dimension. Add to this the whole new world of background adventure, with even Himalayan 'firsts' almost commonplace, and it is small wonder that today's qualifications demand a far different scrutiny.

The hotel meets of the club at New Year and Easter, and of course the annual dinner, became special highlights of the calendar. Even now after long years it is a real pleasure to recall the genuinely friendly welcomes afforded by senior members. Some of the latter were real 'characters', or so at least it seemed to me: the Rev A.E. Robertson, first to complete all the Munros, quietly seated by the hotel log fire, suddenly bursting into lyrical verse in praise, I think, of Slioch; Percy Unna, outstretched on the fireside rug, drinking his ritual six cups of bedtime tea brewed in his own special china teapot; Stuart Jack, 'official' singer of the club song *Oh, my big hobnailers!* at every annual dinner; Willie Ling and George Glover, former presidents and once a 'tiger' partnership on innumerable fine rock-routes in the Northern Highlands; Rooke Corbett, bearded and tall, so tall in fact that he had to have two bars to strengthen the frame of his huge green bicycle.

Attendance at meets, even if sometimes necessarily brief, was always immensely enjoyable. From Crianlarich or Inveroran to Tomdoun or Kinlochewe or Inchnadamph there was never any lack of novelty or interest. The future seemed to be stretching ahead of me with possibilities unlimited. Then, unexpectedly, came a hiccup – a new job took me south.

East Anglia could hardly be described as mountaineer's dream country and when I had to work in Norwich for a year, I found no great cause for rejoicing. The fact that at that time my only means of transport was an ageing bicycle was not an added help.

In the event things were better than I had expected – or doubtless deserved. A foray or two by night to find compensation in climbing some of the local railway signals having failed to satisfy, I looked for better things elsewhere. The 'playgrounds' of Derbyshire seemed to offer the best hopes reasonably near and I managed to persuade one or two friends who actually possessed cars that they would find visits to the Black Rocks, at Cromford, to Brassington with its wonderful honeycombed limestone and even to Laddow (twice) up near Sheffield, experiences of a lifetime. It is good to feel quite sure that they did.

Rather more ambitiously I 'escaped' with my brother and a tent for a weekend in North Wales. Colin had already sampled a number of good climbing days South of the Border – in the Lake District on some of the well known Langdale routes as well as on several of the 'classics' in Snowdonia. I had often heard him tell of these exploits and was not exactly sorry to find myself being whisked westwards to Pen-y-Gwryd and a good campsite near to the hotel.

Our first day was spent, not surprisingly, on Tryfan, on one or two Milestone variations followed by Gashed Crag. Next day it was Lliwedd and all the enjoyment of Route II, giving us fair excuse for a mammoth evening dinner in the hotel.

So far so good. But, bedded down later, sleep came slowly. Indeed, as a rising wind started to fling wild blatters of rain against the tent wall, sleep didn't come at all. Instead, with midnight past and no least let-up, we knew real tremors of anxiety. By two the gale had reached a fever pitch of ferocity, sheets of rain drenching the tent. No doubt now what the outcome was to be; quite philosophically we got busy packing our gear. At four it happened and matter of factly we picked ourselves up out of the sodden mess of fabric. Then we shivered our way to the only shelter available – the outside hotel 'Gents'. It was a long wait until opening time.

Another memorable weekend – with a more cheerful ending – was when a Norwich friend very generously gave me the loan of a car for the whole of the Easter break. The call to head for Scotland was irresistible: I wasted no time in taking the long road north. Next day, with Colin and Iain Jack, we made for Glencoe in a diamond sparkle of early April sunshine. The snow on the tops was in ideal condition and an east-west traverse of the Aonach Eagach gave us of its best. Maybe it was that everything was just right – snow, weather, company – yet in it too was the pleasure of startling contrast to the flats of Norfolk, to which reluctantly I had to hurry back the following day. However that may be, it was certainly the most enjoyable of all the occasions on which I have been along that delectable Glencoe ridge. The day itself was not long enough by half.

NEW HEIGHTS

My first experience of Ben Nevis, also at Easter, three years previously in 1934, had been tragically different. Colin had been up the Ben before, so, after a night in the Glen Nevis hostel, we waded the river and crossed over the ridge to do Carn Mor Dearg and the arête leading to the more interesting approach up the steep eastern snow-slope. That day the Ben was literally swarming with climbers – it was in the middle of an English club meet at Fort William and southern accents were to be heard in plenty; in No.2 Gully alone there was a queue of nine at one time, garlanded with many coils of rope. With us all went well until we were past the summit and half-way down the ordinary path at Lochan Meall an t-Suidhe. There we heard that there had been a serious accident – two well-known English climbers, Colin Kirkus and Maurice Linnell, had fallen while climbing The Castle and the latter had been killed. My brother and I offered to go back up and do what we could to assist, but we were told that this would be pointless; there were already many more than enough helpers to cope with such stretcher work as would be necessary. We would much rather have been able to do something however inadequate, but it was not to be; we just had to accept a particularly sad ending to our day.

In due course we came to know the north face of the Ben at first hand. Occasionally we stayed at the Charles Inglis Clark memorial hut, placed so usefully below the crags beside the Allt a' Mhuillin. My first plod up to it from Fort William was, I recall, alongside a mule hired to carry a more useful load than just our rucksacks. No helicopter uplift in those days.

Our winter visits were mostly in the far back gully-climbing era, usually – memory suggests – in weather wild, wet or worse. In summer the Tower Ridge has always been particularly enjoyable, especially well remembered from almost 60 years back for a speedy, light-hearted romp up and down late one September afternoon. No doubt the Ridge is thought of nowadays as not much more than a good scramble, but however that may be, for me at least it has always been high among my favourites.

Another favourite was the Great Ridge of Garbh Bheinn, which we visited occasionally. Unfortunately, situated as it is in Ardgour, Garbh Bheinn is not so readily accessible, and it was very much more often to the popular routes on the Buachaille or Bidein nam Bian and its outlying tops that we turned our attention.

In recent years critics have occasionally been inclined to write off the thirties as lean and uninspired so far as adventurous climbing was concerned. Such criticism is neither fair nor accurate. Admittedly those were days before the winter 'explosion' took place, that opening up of an almost overwhelming number of original snow and ice routes, many of the highest degree of severity and often on hills which previously had seemed lacking in interest.

Yet I can vouch for the fact that in those distant thirties there was a vast wealth of enthusiasm. And much 'success' too, as the records testify. For example, interest in the various attempts to breach the defences of the Buachaille's Rannoch Wall was particularly intense; when eventually, in 1934, Route 1 was climbed, it was hailed as a truly significant breakthrough. And no wonder. Within two years it was followed by Agag's Groove, nowadays so popular that it can be virtually queued out. A whole new pattern had been set. Also on Buachaille the very severe Direct Route to complete The Chasm had been achieved in 1931, the same year as two of a trio of new routes on Central Buttress. The first ascent of the Mitre Ridge on Beinn a' Bhuird played a major part in attracting more attention to the Cairngorms. On Ben Nevis Graham Macphee was more than busy checking on material for the new edition of the *Guide* which he was editing, while his great rival J.H.B. Bell was equally occupied with the first problems of the great Orion Face. In fact all of this widespread pioneering was being done not just by one or two individuals but by many different enthusiasts. These could hardly be called unadventurous times. There was any amount of inspiration and encouragement for those who were still able to get away to the hills with any great regularity after the outbreak of the war and who were free to open up exciting new possibilities for the future.

Chapter Six

TO THE ALPS
1938 AND 1939

F OR the mountain maniac nurtured on Edward Whymper and Leslie Stephen, Mummery and Geoffrey Winthrop Young, a first visit to the Alps may fairly be said to be an all-time peak of enjoyment.

For Colin and me, though, late July 1938 looked like proving to be one notable exception.

Overnight Glasgow–London, economy long-sea crossing Newhaven–Dieppe and a night of third class wooden-seated rail travel was a doubtful beginning; we arrived at Saas Fee dry-eyed and dog weary. A quick change in the hut of a friendly mule driver was followed by a long, long slog up a steep, sweat-larded path to the Mischabel Hut at 10,000ft plus. There we drew breath and compared headaches as we joined Graham Macphee, fellow SMC member and alpinist of no mean repute. The gloom in his greeting was unmistakable. He had come up to the hut in fast time the previous day, was just back from climbing the Lenzspitze, Nadelhorn and Ulrichshorn – and was being violently sick. As Colin and I both felt similarly incommoded after only a few mouthfuls of soup, we voted our first evening in a high Swiss hut a conspicuous non-success. In fact we agreed that the best thing to do would be to retreat ingloriously to the valley next day.

Fortunately Graham was of sterner stuff – so stern indeed that he had us out of our blankets before three the next morning, unselfishly agreeing to take us up the Ulrichshorn (12,890ft) – his second ascent in two days.

Apart from the glacier crossing it was all like a homely winter Munro, with a snow-blade of a ridge whipped by an icy wind. The grey-blue and pink dawn gave promise of more sunshine to come; only beyond the depths of the valley a huge bronze cloud-anvil above the Portjengrat was stabbed and stabbed again by fierce flashes of lightning. We were back at the hut by seven and within minutes clattering down the steep zigzags to Saas and relaxation over second breakfast.

The main part of our programme was due to start two days later at the Weissmies Hut, on the east side of the Saastal. Colin and I had joined the Swiss Alpine Club and with three other Scots, including Graham Macphee, were to be taking part in a *semaine clubistique* of the Diablerets Section. This would, our bulletin informed us, take in some half dozen first-class peaks, all for a cost rather less than the tariff for a guided ascent of the Matterhorn. It looked a good bargain to us.

At the Weissmies Hut – a more varied and relaxed climb from the valley – we met up with the Swiss contingent and the other Scots, John Brown and Tom MacKinnon, both strong climbers, the latter to be a member 17 years later of the first successful Kangchenjunga expedition.

It was to be another 36 hours before Colin and I really started to enjoy ourselves. For Day One we were together on the same *cordée*, led by a middle-aged Swiss who made no great secret of doubting our competence. The programme was introductory – rock work on the Schwarzmies, an airy whale-back edge. Our leader insisted on our roping up during the approach, a precaution adopted by none of the other parties, whereas on several exposed perches later on, when I paused to safeguard Colin, I was berated by the Führer for being too slow. Fortunately we did not have to endure the same partnership again.

Thereafter all went more than ordinarily well. Amends were made in the next two days, when we climbed three good peaks – Fletschhorn (13,126ft), Laquinhorn (13,140ft) and Weissmies (13,224ft). At 4,001 metres, by no more than the height of the cairn, the Fletschhorn just managed to squeeze into the august company of Alpine *quatre mille mètres* summits. Sadly, however, it was fated to be demoted later on to below the magic level – reminiscent of our own hills and the way in which Sir Hugh Munro's sacrosanct 'Tables' have been so ignominiously topped and tailed by metrication.

The traverse of the Weissmies was particularly enjoyable, with splendid dawn views back across the Saastal to the Dom and Täschhorn. The morning's work was almost entirely on snow and as our place in the caravan was well to the rear, by the time we had reached the final barrier wall, the steps ahead looked as though they had been stamped out by a battalion of abominable snowmen. Thereafter, on the descent, I well remember the longest, most exhilarating swoop of a standing glissade I have ever enjoyed.

It was on the Weissmies that we experienced two other 'firsts'. In a sheltered hollow beyond the summit we came on the rest of the party engaged in an orgy of raw egg sucking. Colin and I were still unused to this apparently time-honoured Swiss custom and we watched fascinated. The ritual is of course simplicity itself: a playful tap with each end of the egg on the pick of the ice-axe and a gurgle of satisfaction as the mouthful is disposed of, then a smack of the lips and all is over. We tried it ourselves in due course, but it must be said that we accounted for few of the 360 eggs consumed during the week; we preferred to risk the doubtful properties of our tinned meat, ominously labelled *Hackbraten*.

Then after the snack the Swiss sang, while the sun warmed us genially and the clouds played tricks with the views. All joined in spontaneously and with obvious enjoyment. How often during the course of our week together were we to hear *Aimons nos montagnes, nos Alpes de neige…* sung on the tops and in the huts! And how well the singing always fitted in with our own exuberant mood!

Our reward was an off-day of sun-basking at the Almageleralp, though there were regrets too, as we missed out on what was evidently a fine traverse of the Portjengrat, enjoyed by most of the Swiss. Our consciences suffered further twinges when, in the late afternoon, we descended to the Saastal fleshpots for a night and morning of luxury. As climax to this decadence and before setting off once more, the five Scots – regularly referred to by the Swiss as 'les Anglais' – provided a litre of wine at lunch for all to celebrate, apparently in traditional fashion, the new boys' achievement in having reached 4,000 metres for the first time.

The second half of the *semaine clubistique* was to take us by way of the Britannia Hut to the finish at Zermatt. There were to be good things on each day's programme and, despite the lunch, we set off jauntily enough uphill on the four-hour climb to the hut.

We were now back to serious business. Next item was the Rimpfischhorn (13,785ft), highest summit of the week and promising a day to remember. For it the 'tigers' of the party, with an east-west traverse as their choice, had to be up at 1.30am; the remaining lesser mortals, bound for the easier 'back door' approach, were allowed an extra hour of luxury.

Our route across the much-crevassed glacier took us below the south face of the Allalinhorn to the high Allalin Pass beyond. And there before us, unforgettably, was a fantastic first view of Zermatt *vier Tausender* – Weisshorn, Ober Gabelhorn, Dent Blanche, Matterhorn – more majestic, more impressive than ever we could have imagined.

Above the col a wide snow-saucer and steeper wall beyond led to an easy rock scramble and the summit. This last belvedere was not exactly roomy, with seating accommodation which suggested dangling one's legs over the fiercely perpendicular east face – 'a wide front of sombre and unstable precipice,' so described and first ascended by Geoffrey Winthrop Young. We had not been there long when we were joined by the ridge party, who seemed well pleased with their work.

Back on the glacier on the downward return route to the hut, we found the snow softening fast in the morning heat. The crevasses seemed to be gasping, mouths agape, and once Colin put a leg through a fragile snow-bridge, to be held on the rope and jerked back to safety like a trout from a burn. I was finding the glare and the altitude thoroughly unpleasant and, with a thumping headache, was glad to reach the sanctuary of the hut. Fortunately, despite the sun's vindictiveness, all was well by evening and the supper spaghetti mountain was a meal to be savoured. Thereafter the Swiss were unusually vocal and even prevailed upon the Scots quintet to sing. The applause was politely cordial; the request was not repeated.

Sadly for the final two days of the meet the weather played up. During a rock-climbing morning on the lower-level Egginergrat storm-clouds were building up, and although there was no immediate setback, it was obvious that trouble was brewing for the afternoon. So, in fact, it proved. Rain, hail and thunder launched a venomous onslaught and we were glad to be safely housed back at the Britannia.

Thanks to this hostile weather, the week's climax was not as good as it might have been. We had to be away at 2 o'clock for the long day ahead – over the Adler Pass, up the

Strahlhorn (13,749ft) and down to Zermatt. To begin with, fresh snow on the glacier made the going doubly tedious, the crevasses harder to detect. (Colin and I were on a rope with a more than generously built Swiss and did not relish the possibility of having to hoist him from unplumbed depths). A bitter wind welcomed us to the col and did nothing to stifle the anarchy already abroad at the sight of mist thickly blanketing our peak. Most of the Swiss were for giving the climb a miss, but fortunately the experience of much Munro-bagging in similar conditions prevailed and all but two trooped obediently with us up and down in a damp couple of hours.

A nasty descent from the pass, partially on new snow on ice, brought us to the badly crevassed Adlergletscher, thence at last to the more friendly woods and meadows and first scattered chalets of Zermatt. Fourteen hours after leaving the Britannia Hut we sat down in the Café Chemin de Fer. We drank to the health of our Swiss friends, then escorted them to the station, where at 6 o'clock the train rattled them away, their cheery goodbyes still in our ears, thoughts of the grand week we had shared with them uppermost in our minds.

Macphee had to follow them the next morning, leaving the remnant foursome to a rather uninspiring day of heel-kicking. Between spells of overeating we managed to identify one or two of the more celebrated guides, though this pastime hardly made up for the morbid hour spent contemplating the Matterhorn relics in the museum.

Another day later life regained its brighter hue – a move this time to the Bétemps Hut for an attempt on Monte Rosa. On the way up we were not too happy with the weather, with storm-clouds forming and reforming round the spire of the Matterhorn, while on a brief evening reconnaissance mist and the threat of rain had driven us back to the hut. We could only hope that these portents and the barometer were conspiring to lie shamelessly.

Our morning welcome as we left the hut was no more encouraging – low cloud and warm, lifeless air. However, we were prepared if necessary to accept defeat higher up and for the time being we plodded mechanically onwards to the edge of the upper glacier, where we paused to put on the rope. As we fumbled in the darkness, we heard the deep thunder of an avalanche pouring from the neighbouring Lyskamm, its menace intensified by the breathlessness of the night.

Work among the crevasses of the glacier required all our attention, so that we scarcely noticed the gradual lightening of the sky or the stars glimpsed occasionally through the thinning stratum of cloud. The temperature too had dropped. Imperceptibly ridges and pinnacles were taking shape in the growing daylight.

Then suddenly we paused. The pageant of dawn had begun. At our feet a grey sea of cloud engulfed the lower peaks and valleys, but in the distance the spires of the Alpine giants were touched by the rising sun. From the Weisshorn to the Matterhorn each in turn caught the light till it seemed as if we alone on Monte Rosa were still in shadow.

Bernese Oberland neighbours: Schreckhorn and Lauteraarhorn beyond the Unteraar glacier.

It was to be long enough before we too enjoyed the welcome sunshine – a hard slog up a long snowfield where even the most violent step-kicking could not save fingers and toes from the misery of what was now keen frost. Then suddenly we stepped into brilliant warmth and we awakened to a fuller consciousness.

We became aware of the other parties on the mountain – the two fast-moving Swiss, the German and his wife, cheery and competent, the methodical old guide and his pessimistic client who had protected himself against every possible turn of the weather with snow goggles, balaclava helmet, felt hat, and even a broad white handkerchief to shield the back of his neck.

The final ridge had looked comparatively short, but distance had deceived us and we did not reach the summit for another two hours. A steep snow and ice slope was followed by rocks reminiscent of the Aonach Eagach in Glencoe and a second, steeper snow tower, then rocks again culminating in an ice-layered chimney.

Hard work it was and we were rather light-headed at the altitude of 15,000ft, but nonetheless an airy sun-warmed crest provided the climb with an unforgettable climax.

In the shade of the huge cairn the two Swiss and a party of four Italians who had come over the jagged frontier top were already resting and eating, and we were not reluctant to follow their example. From our vantage-point at the highest of Monte Rosa's tops – the Dufourspitze (15,216ft and our altitude record) – the whole vast bulk of the mountain was within our ken, a complex picture of black and white against a grey background of clouds reaching far over Piedmont and the plain of Lombardy.

Our descent, begun a short hour later, was anything but banal. In the iced chimney we watched the old guide, a model of unruffled competence, pilot his Herr to safer ground at the end of a very short rope. On the slope above the col lower down, where the sun had loosened the covering of snow, we were glad enough to be roped ourselves.

But once these difficulties were over we made quicker time and soon were running the gauntlet of a trough between unstable-looking ice seracs. The sun, however, was not yet strong enough to send any of these pinnacles crashing across our path, and it was only when we were resting once again beyond the heat and glare of the glacier that we heard any sounds of afternoon bombardment.

Then it was a mere walk to the hut; or rather it was a race, for the thought of many cups of tea was uppermost in our minds. Fourteen hours after our departure in the darkness we were lying outstretched in the sunshine, sleepily tracing the cloud-patterns on the distant cathedral spire of the Matterhorn.

The sunshine, unfortunately, did not last long beyond our return to Zermatt. The other half of our Scots quartet had to go home, leaving Colin and me on our own with bright ideas and no bright weather to match. Heavily laden we trailed up to the Schönbühl Hut, but with drearily low cloud and rain, plans for both a guided ascent of the Dent Blanche and a crossing of the Col Durand to Zinal had to be abandoned.

TO THE ALPS

So we had to be content with Monte Rosa as our climax. But, after all, why not? Heading home, we were very much more than just ordinarily content.

*****

In the summer of 1939 continental Europe was no happy playground. Munich was past, but certainly not the build-up of the Nazi menace. Few doubted that those were sultry days of waiting before the breaking of the storm.

I had the chance nevertheless to make my escape from Glasgow at the tail end of July, sadly this time on my own as Colin was not free. My intention was to join once again in the Diablerets Section meet, that year in the Oberland, and I had to rendezvous at the hospice at the Grimsel Pass.

The early stages of my traveller's tale had in them little of note, only unhurried enjoyment. Then, in Grindelwald I began to get the feel of the Alps once again. A rather dreary cloud-base gave way to steadily brightening weather, and a late afternoon walk up the Faulhorn introduced me to an Oberland panorama in superb low-sun colouring. Particularly impressive were the views of the Wetterhorn and Eiger north walls. The Eiger Nordwand had in fact been climbed for the first time the previous summer by two Germans and two Austrians, thus winning for Hitler the desperate 'death or glory' race for Germany he had so set his heart on.

Next morning I passed under the rock-bastions of the Wetterhorn on a fiercely hot walk to the Grosse Scheidegg. Beyond, the descent was less trying; then by way of Schwarzwaldalp and Meiringen I enjoyed the luxury of some spectacular bus travel up to the Grimsel.

Early breakfast in the morning allowed time to spare before the others arrived, so I made a brisk ascent of the Klein Siedelhorn (9,082ft), a snow-brindled peak above the pass reminiscent of some Munro in Knoydart or Glen Affric: grass and moorland, boulders and troughs of snow, finally a ridge entirely of snow – all enjoyable and very warm. At the cairn I was joined by a solitary Swiss, but either he was unusually taciturn or else he wanted to be alone, for our conversation died an untimely death and, leaving him to his meditations, I was soon rattling down a mostly friendly ridge.

Myself apart, Tom MacKinnon and Graham Macphee were the only ones of 'les Anglais' of 1938 to join the meet, but I was delighted to find myself greeting some half a dozen old friends among the Swiss. We proceeded to sit down to a more than ample lunch, no doubt unwise preparation for the walk of four and a bit hours to the Lauteraar Hut.

The programme for the week was, I think, rather less attractive than that of the previous year. There was, of course, the inevitable patch of bad weather, but it would hardly be fair to claim that any fault lay there. Rather it was that there was over-much time spent on tramping from hut to hut, on a rather tame route up the grey and red rock bluff of the Hühnerstock (10,893ft) and on a thirsty crossing of the Strahlegg Pass. Yet perhaps it is just because so much of the week fell so flat that the two 'big' days – Schreckhorn and Finsteraarhorn – stand out the more brilliantly as dazzling peaks to remember.

Our base for these two climbs, the Strahlegg Hut, has a superb situation above the Grindelwald Glacier: facing it are the Finsteraarhorn, Agassizhorn, Fiescherhörner and Pfaffenstöckli, an array of high summits remote and ethereal as we first saw them in the mists of late afternoon; behind, the Schreckhorn, as remote and seemingly as unattainable.

I think it was almost certainly at the Strahlegg Hut, when I dossed down on my mattress for the night, that I found I was to be sleeping next to Josef Knubel, Geoffrey Winthrop Young's famous guide. Maybe I wished him 'Good night' or, less likely, 'Good morning'; however that may be, to have conversed with 'Little J' is undoubtedly my greatest claim to Alpine fame.

It was in 1861 that the Schreckhorn (13,385ft) was climbed for the first time, last of the Oberland 'four thousanders' to fall to the pioneers. Early descriptions of the achievement did nothing to minimise the threat in its name, Peak of Terror. The 15 exacting hours and two high bivouacs involved in that first ascent earned honourable mention in a chapter entitled 'How to Get Killed in the Alps'. Another exulted in full, lurid detail: 'We were frequently flattened out against the rocks, like beasts of ill repute nailed to a barn, with fingers and toes inserted into four different cracks which tested the elasticity of our frames to the uttermost.' Or later, as the party neared the summit: 'The scene was in itself significant enough for men of weak nerves. Taking a drop of brandy all round, we turned to the assault.' Dramatic stuff indeed.

Even in more recent times the the late Frank Smythe gave a vivid account of a thunderstorm following a wild dawn and weird green sunrise, which nearly brought disaster high on the peak's south-west ridge. The party was within 500ft of the summit when the storm assailed them 'with an insane squall of hail and tremendous cracks of thunder.' Then, lower down as they retreated, it returned with renewed fury and the wind was so violent that there was a danger of being blown off the mountain. 'Our chances of survival were nil if things went on as they did.' Then miraculously the storm moderated.*

As we clattered upstairs to our mattresses in the Strahlegg Hut, we could hardly help wondering what kind of welcome the Peak of Terror had in store for us next day.

Fortunately there was no ominous green sunrise, only moonlight giving way to the gold and silver promise of a perfect day. Above an initial sleepy trudge up screes and snow-patches, a complex glacier world of crevasses and jumbled ice seracs brought us to the wide snow couloir we were to follow. This had the look of a really treacherous avalanche-chute in the wrong kind of weather or even later in the day, but as we found them the snow conditions were ideal. The angle, not surprisingly, steepened the higher we climbed, but no

Highest of the Oberland peaks, Finsteraarhorn (14,026ft).

* Smythe, F.S. *Climbs and Ski Runs* Blackwood, 1931

desperate axe-work was needed, not a stone fell to shake our peace of mind. It all might well have been Beinn Laoigh's Central Gully multiplied several times over.

High above, at the corniced exit, we paused, suddenly buffeted by an icy wind. We now faced the most enjoyable problem of the day, a Cuillin sequence of airy rock towers and turrets with, in between, snow-blades sharp enough to demand suitably delicate treading. And then it was the summit itself – a shapely dome of snow with a friendly welcome.

In the keen wind the air was particularly clear, the visibility very special. Glacier seas, edged with reefs and promontories, stretched away at our feet; near at hand the Wetterhorn and Lauteraarhorn half-hid the Engadine, far behind; all the Oberland peaks, not least of interest Eiger, Mönch and Jungfrau; a more distant catalogue – Monte Rosa, Matterhorn, Weisshorn, Dent Blanche, Mont Blanc. It seemed as though we were looking at the outspread map of the Alps, specially beautified in contour and colour. We had been provided indeed with a feast of enjoyment.

Yet some hours later we stopped not far above the hut to look back at our route. Even as we gazed, a light cloud drifted across the face of the mountain at half height leaving the upper pyramid remote and inaccessible. Already the reality of its rocks and snows was fading; already the old impressions were beginning to return.

As it was considered, on safety grounds, that the chosen route up the next day's peak, the Finsteraarhorn, should allow of only two ropes of three, a spirit of competitiveness inevitably reared its head. In the end, three Swiss and the three '*Anglais*' – Macphee, MacKinnon and myself – were selected, much of course to our delight, the Finsteraarhorn at 4,275 metres (14,026ft) being the highest peak in the Oberland and the day's alternative, the Gross Fiescherhorn, no desperately close rival.

The only fly in the ointment was that, having been accorded this honour, we would have to justify the choice. Macphee, as rope leader, was at pains to point this out; the honour of Scotland, he maintained, was at stake. I had better, he kindly hinted, make sure that my socks were duly pulled up. I retired to my bunk fearing that patriotism would definitely not be enough.

At breakfast my worst fears seemed to be fully justified. The Swiss had clearly decided that this was an unnecessary frivolity and were already fidgeting at the door. I could achieve no more than a flustered gulp of coffee before seizing my rucksack and stumbling out into the night.

At first it was very dark and I can remember no more than a blurred succession of snow-slopes and rock outcrops as we slanted upwards to strike the glacier above the tangle of the ice-fall. There we paused briefly to rope up, as the moon came up to create the usual uncanny lighting effects in the unreal world about us.

Suddenly it was only too real. Far above us in the Agassiz couloir, which we were about to climb, we heard it: 'Attention! Pierres!' In seconds we were crouching in our steps, heads tucked down in safety. It was a fusillade of stones sent down by a party of two already high on the rocks above and passing with the proverbial whine of angry hornets. Only Tom was struck, fortunately taking the blow on his axe-shaft, and although his arm was numb for some time afterwards, he lost none of his habitual equanimity.

Except for a patch of ice some 200 feet up, the first part of the couloir was good firm snow and gave no excuse for a slackening of pace. Nor did the islands of rock higher up. From snow to rock and rock to snow the Swiss trio wound their lively way with Scotland hard on their heels. Mindful too of our own experience, we spared an occasional thought for another party below and trod with particular delicacy.

On the Agassizjoch we met the sun and with it a bitter wind. Here if anywhere was the place to shelter and eat second breakfast; even a biscuit and mouthful of tea would be better than nothing. But no; there was much more work to come and seconds were still precious. 'We gnaw the nail of hurry. Master, away!' And so perforce I had to keep going, like some piece of clockwork; only the clockwork was beginning to feel in need of being wound up.

The final ridge of the Finsteraarhorn springs up from the Agassizjoch to the summit in three gigantic bounds, all of roughly equal height and totalling nearly 1,400 feet. For the first we had rock to cope with and we were soon playing a genial game of follow-my-leader up and over and round a disarray of blocks reminiscent of Skye. Then came a pause, not, alas! for breath or refreshment, but to put on our crampons; ahead an ice-slope curled upwards like a wind-filled sail to make step number two.

Again the angle eased off for the brief respite of the Hugisattel, and again steepened into its ultimate fling of rocks and snow. Then, when I was beginning to feel that another stretch really would have me on my knees, suddenly we were at the cairn.

Even then, however, our stay was none of your usual jolly Swiss affairs. Hand-shaking there may have been, but there was not even a half-hearted chorus and certainly no basking in the sun – the shrivelling wind saw emphatically to that. Our time for the ascent had been 5 hours 40 minutes and I certainly was willing to believe, as we learned afterwards, that it was the second fastest of the season.

On the return journey to the hut we were to take almost exactly seven hours. The descent to the Agassizjoch demanded back-breaking concentration on the ice-slope and constant care on the rocks which, with others directly below, seemed as loose as a scree-run. In the long couloir, too, where the snow had deteriorated, much step-cutting was needed in underlying ice. It was a relief indeed when we were all finally reunited below all major difficulty.

The sky meanwhile had clouded over, although the obvious bad weather held off for the time being and we had only the treacly snow to contend with on the final walk back to the hut. There we were pleasantly surprised to find we were ahead of the Fiescherhorn party. It had been a tremendous day and Scotland's honour had certainly remained unsullied, but I could not help feeling that the sparing of even another half hour for our uphill race would have added still more to the sum total of our enjoyment.

Mist, rain and heavy snow duly arrived and went on to try our patience for three full days. Sadly this ended the meet in anti-climax, and a none-too-pleasant descent was duly made to Grindelwald, where we said final farewells to our Swiss friends.

Hopes, nevertheless, were still high with our Scottish threesome, so the following morning we took the first train up to the Jungfraujoch. The weather by this time was showing signs of relenting, but it was not until the early afternoon that we were able to benefit. Macphee had set our sights on the Trugberg, a peak he had not done before and which would involve a climb of only 1,562 feet above the 11,342 feet of the Jungfraujoch. A glacier crossing of 50 minutes, now in the full glare of the sun, took us below the glittering south face of the Mönch to the saddle of the Obermönchjoch, but on the first rocks of the Trugberg it was very soon obvious that with so great an accumulation of new snow, defeat would be inevitable. We returned therefore to the pass and although it was now after four o'clock and clouds were again massing, we set about climbing the Mönch (13,468ft).

Working fast and pausing seldom, we needed no more than another hour for the now familiar mix of rocks and snow. Indeed, with the Jungfraujoch start, I would imagine the Mönch to be the easiest four thousander in the Alps. Yet despite the shortness of the climb and the fact that once more bad weather clamped down on our final trudge to the hotel, our satisfaction knew no bounds.

My companions stayed on at the Jungfraujoch, but it was a further three days before the Jungfrau was in condition – and a great day they had of it. By then, as work was calling, I was on my way back home to Scotland. It was a comfortable journey, though perhaps I suffered from a slightly stiff neck, craning to look back at the Wetterhorn and Eiger, trying to prolong to the last my goodbye.

Four weeks later we were at war.

Chapter Seven

5TH BATTALION – 1940

THE brief, bizarre life of the 5th (Special Reserve) Battalion Scots Guards makes an episode in the annals of British military history that is quite remarkably unique. When, early in 1940, the War Office issued an appeal for volunteers with skiing and mountaineering experience, the response was immediate and enthusiastic. To Bordon, near Aldershot, came men from many parts: Scotsmen, Englishmen, Welshmen, Irishmen, Canadians, South Africans, even, it was rumoured, two Russian princes. From the Army, the RAF, the Navy and civilian life they came: men from the BEF in France, men who had served in Palestine or on the North-West Frontier, Sandhurst men, Varsity men, pilots and yachtsmen, cooks and lumberjacks, gunners and signallers, tradesmen and Etonians. And, certainly not least, there were the illustrious few who had won reputations in Greenland, on Everest and, more obviously, in the winter sports arenas of Switzerland.

The formation of the battalion had been undertaken by the Brigade of Guards, clearly with much misgiving. This was not altogether surprising, for it was no natural child that was being adopted and its future, to say the least, was uncertain. To ensure that discipline would not be entirely lacking, one company was drawn from the Scots Guards proper and there were certainly many occasions on which the wisdom of this move was justified. Otherwise, all who volunteered had to agree to serve, if need be, as ordinary guardsmen. As it said above the dotted line: 'In the interests of the service, and at the request of the Army Council, I volunteer to serve in any capacity with the special unit or units referred to in War Office U.P.T. 8236 (A.G.1.a) dated 17th January, 1940. For this purpose I am willing to relinquish my present war substantive or substantive rank and status as a warrant or non-commissioned officer temporarily upon the following terms…' Willingly, almost eagerly, agreement was given. The rank of sergeant was an honour in such a unit.

The extraordinary thing was that no one was quite certain what it was all for. The most obvious explanation was, of course, that the battalion was destined for Finland. The Finnish-Russian war had been raging since the end of the previous November and although the gigantic Russian 'steamroller' had been halted all along the snowbound front, it was by no means certain that the gallant Finnish resistance could hold out much longer. The Press in Britain and indeed in nearly all free countries had from the outset championed Finland's cause and there had been much talk of sending reinforcements of men and materials. So far, however, no action had been taken; the War Cabinet had not seen fit to risk infringing Norwegian and Swedish neutrality, or embarking on open war with Russia.

But there was no knowing what was to be the next move in the grand strategy of the war, and if Finland as destination was a feasible theory, so too were others. Troops trained in skiing and mountaineering could be used as profitably in the Caucasus as on the Greenland ice-cap. The ground was certainly rich enough for rumours to thrive in like weeds.

My own entry into the august ranks of the Brigade of Guards took place on 23 February. I had travelled south the previous night from Glasgow, where I happened to be stationed at the time, elated that my application had so far been successful, yet still not risking too much optimism. I was all too aware of my lack of skiing prowess, although obviously everything would depend on what sort of standard was demanded. All I could do was go for interview determined to make the most of my meagre resources. Fortunately the adjutant was a big-hearted man. 'All right,' he conceded, 'you'll do. Though, of course, we wouldn't take anyone with less skiing experience than you.' I hurried out before he could change his mind, then I set off back to Glasgow on 48 hours embarkation leave.

The hustle of these journeyings up and down the country was excellent practice for the days that followed at Quebec Barracks, Bordon, for while we were there we were to have few dull moments. Morning drills and afternoon tactics, zeroing of rifles (the Mark IV with its six-inch bayonet was at that time a novel toy), lectures on Everest and Greenland, and above all interminable issues of kit gave us only rare opportunities to draw breath. Much of the special Arctic equipment, prepared with surprisingly minute care down to the last vital detail, we were shown only at demonstrations – the tents and the sledging gear, the down sleeping-bags and the quilted greatcoats, the gloves and the anoraks, virtually every-thing in white and all looking like the treasure of some polar Aladdin's cave. What the cost of it all must have been we did not pause to consider; that was happily not our concern. Nor, it need hardly be said, were any civilian tax payers invited to attend the shows.

Even though we were kept hard at it during and often after duty hours, the mood of the battalion was altogether light-hearted. These were still days when *Blitzkrieg* was unknown – before Dunkirk and Namsos, Crete and Tobruk and Singapore. It was not difficult, as mere guardsmen or junior NCOs, to forget responsibility for a while and take to the more congenial pastime of clowning; certainly the fun in barrack-room and canteen grew more and more boisterous as the days went past. No doubt many a regular guardsman was filled with horror to see so much flippancy in these sacred precincts, or to hear the popular refrain of our first theme-song, an adaptation of *Old King Cole* which ended:

'Double, double, double, double, double,' said the subalterns;
'Move to the right in threes,' said to the sergeants;
'Left, right, left, right, left,' said the corporals;
'Beer, beer, beer,' said the guardsmen,
'Merry, merry men are we;
'There's none so fair as can compare
'With the Scottish Alpini.'

Quite the most remarkable thing, however, was the ceaseless undercurrent of speculation. From morning till night, day in day out, there was no escape from it. Security was as strict as the blackout; we were not allowed even a glimmer of reliable information, and this went for the immediate future as well as for our more distant fate. The most popular theory was always that we were to go to Chamonix and train there with the Chasseurs Alpins, but there were plenty of pessimists to argue that this was mere wishful thinking.

We were not in fact kept in suspense for long. February went out in a flurry of activity and it was obvious on 1 March that the climax had arrived. With fitting pomp and ceremony the battalion was paraded on the square preparatory to an inspection and march-past, then mustered in the gym for a final exhortation to avoid the cardinal sin – blotting the illustrious copybook of the Brigade of Guards. Next morning, whistling and singing at the rising sun, we were off.

C.E. Montague it was who described so vividly that prerogative of private soldiers travelling in wartime – the feeling of being 'free to the uttermost'. Only to them, he says, 'does the real magic carpet come with sealed orders to carry them Heaven knows whither – to any part of any continent of them all.' Such indeed was our mood that sunny March morning.

Our magic carpet duly wafted us to Southampton, thus giving the lie to those rumour-mongers who had tipped Gourock or Invergordon. Out into the vast embarkation shed we tumbled and there sat on our kits, happily eating mutton-pies, till our turn came to go aboard the waiting *Ulster Prince*. The official wheels seemed to be turning with unwonted precision, for there was remarkably little delay and we were pleasantly surprised to find that the three-bunk cabins to which we were directed were expected to hold only four. Our company, Left Flank, must have been the last to embark, for it was not long afterwards that the *Ulster Prince* moved slowly out into Southampton Water and took up station inside the boom. As we waited on deck for the sun to set, the scene about us looked unbelievably peaceful. Had it not been for the two or three destroyers and the remote barrage balloons, this might well have seemed the start of some commonplace evening cruise. Then frosty darkness fell and it was with reluctance that we turned from watching searchlights criss-crossing the starlit dome of sky. When next we came on deck it was full daylight again and we were safely inside the defences of Le Havre.

I have clear memories of only two incidents during the remainder of the long journey to Chamonix – for it was indeed thither that we were being transported. The first is of a picture of our platoon – tail-end as usual – hot, weary, dishevelled and not a little mutinous after six hours' toil unloading stores and equipment from the *Ulster Prince*, doubling down the platform of Le Havre station and piling helter-skelter into already bursting compartments, just as the train was drawing out.

The second incident occurred somewhere along the line, probably not far from Paris.

The train was indulging in one of its interminable and inexplicable halts and happened to be standing opposite a long row of goods wagons. Strict orders had been issued forbidding anyone to leave his carriage, but continental railway architecture being what it is, temptation proved too strong and an enterprising fellow passenger decided to investigate. As he climbed across and entered the wagon, we watched fascinated; then, after an age of suspense, he returned in triumph – bearing aloft four bottles of wine.

Chamonix gave us a welcome of almost embarrassing warmth. This was the first time that British troops had visited the town and the good people fairly let themselves go. On the station platform we were met by a bevy of girls, dressed for the occasion in national red, white and blue, who bore down upon us with cups of excellent coffee and baskets full of croissants. This gave us a foretaste of what was to come. As we moved out of the station a band of the Chasseurs kept playing the *Marseillaise* and *God Save the King* at regular intervals – a commendably patriotic gesture, if rather a hindrance to smooth progress. However, we eventually passed out of the musicians' range and reached the street. Here we were greeted by the rest of the populace, thronging the pavements under an impressive archway of flags and bunting.

No doubt the applause for the first companies to leave the station was really rousing, for even in our position at the rear we did remarkably well. There is certainly a fine feeling of satisfaction to be cheered to the echo merely for having arrived in a winter sports resort on a free skiing holiday.

It is, however, another aspect of our welcome that I think of now with most pleasure. During the leisurely railway climb from St Gervais the clouds had been down, grey, sombre, rather depressing. But as we clattered out into the more bracing air of Chamonix itself, the curtain rolled aside slowly and theatrically to reveal the mountains. Thin veils of mist still girdled them at mid-height, but an incredible distance above, their domes and crests of snow, their rock-walls and towers stood crystal clear against the blue spread of the sky. There, unmistakably, were the tumbled ice-falls of Mont Blanc and there, ranged at lower heights, the monarch's courtiers – the *aiguilles*.

This then was Chamonix. Zermatt and the Oberland I had known, and now here I was in the third of the great classic centres. Even if I never saw the Alps again, I could have no grounds for complaint.

Our platoon was allotted billets on the outskirts of the town in what had formerly been a dance hall. This was now bare and bleak inside with only some Frenchly feminine murals left to recall the frenzies of peace. We soon discovered that the floor was both hard and draughty, and the first night we spent on it, before we had been issued with paillasses, was one of questionable comfort. The frost was bitter and set us chittering in our inadequate blankets long before daylight returned. It was almost a pleasure to get up and start chipping the ice from our shaving water.

So far as messing was concerned we looked like being still more unfortunate when, on

Bound for the ski slopes at Chamonix.

the very first evening, the two company cooks saw fit to deviate from the straight and narrow far enough to have themselves arrested. This seemed a great joke until we found out in the morning that they had not been released in time to cook our breakfast. However, either they mended their ways thereafter or else they were replaced by others of a sterner moral fibre, for the cookhouse functioned adequately from that day onward.

Such trials and tribulations served to give added piquancy to our other pleasures. These usually began with the morning parade, a mercifully brief formality outside our billets. As we formed up on the iron-hard snow, the biting frost banished the last traces of sleep, for although the sun was already touching the topmost spires of the *aiguilles*, it would be long enough before it reached the valley. Then we would move off across the fields, skis crunching on the crisp snow-furrows, till we had reached one of the tracks that slanted upwards through the woods. For the rest of the morning and again after lunch-break we would be kept busy on nursery slopes. These were glorious hours, warm and carefree after the sun had thawed us out, and our only complaint was that time passed too quickly. The experts, of course, protested loudly that such practice was unworthy of their skill, but it was strange all the same how thoroughly they always seemed to be enjoying themselves. For my part I found the snow frozen much too hard, and at times it was difficult to believe that I had ever been on skis before.

We were given various tests, always down slalom courses of such steepness that I inevitably came to grief at turn after turn. I felt the threat of being returned to my unit hanging horribly close above my head, and tried in vain to console myself with the reflection that at least I must be better than another guardsman in the platoon, who boasted that his sole claim to skiing proficiency was that he could ride a horse.

However, as day succeeded day, balance and confidence began to return and linked 'Sitzmarks' to give way to less inelegant turns. I even managed – by adding cajolery to a supreme effort of skill – to have myself moved up from the beginners' class. For the moment at least I was safe.

During off-duty spells at lunchtime or in the late afternoon, we would lounge outside the billets, often basking cat-like in the spring sunshine. It was good to sit back, virtuously tired, and gaze across the valley at the long saw-edge of peaks. One of my companions had climbed the Aiguille de l'M in pre-war days and he and I started to lay plans for an assault on it. The fact that he was not quite sure which was the M, or that we lacked maps, ice-axes and even nailed boots, did not deter us and we waited hopefully for an off-day. Unfortunately – or perhaps fortunately – it was never to come; our aiguille-hunting was to get no further than that distant appreciation so aptly expressed by Geoffrey Winthrop Young: 'Theirs are shapes which we did not need to climb to enjoy: among which a mountaineer at rest may read his pleasure from line and mass and shadow and atmosphere as surely as a musician can read harmony from a score without help from hand or ear.'

Another incidental disappointment, for me at least, was that we never had any chance of seeing the Chasseurs at work. On the afternoon following our arrival they had treated us to a most elaborate concert, full of friendliness towards us and working up to a grand final fanfare of regimental music, played on their hunting-horns with traditional accompanying flourishes. This gesture, we thought, hinted at co-operation during the days ahead; but if such was the intention, nothing came of it. I remember watching them moving off one morning, no doubt bound for training manoeuvres, but that was all; not once did I see them on ski. Off duty, of course, they were to be seen on the streets or visiting the various cafés, and several good evenings we spent in their company. What astonished me most was their untidy turn-out and frequent slovenly behaviour. For instance, it came as something of a shock to see a sentry outside their headquarters scrounging a match from his relief in order to light his pipe, while across the street the British guard was being mounted by some of our regular guardsmen as impeccably as if in the shadow of Buckingham Palace. An amusing contrast, though perhaps no more intriguing than would have been that between us had a skiing contest being arranged. Maybe the 'ski experts from Scotland,' as the Paris papers chose to call us, would have come off with less distinction.

It was on a Monday that we had arrived in Chamonix and for the best part of five days – until the following Friday evening – everything was perfect. The combination of sunshine and ideal snow had gone to our heads and the long hours of exercise had brought us to an

Chamonix, March 1940. Queuing for the funicular to the Col de Voza.

exhilarating pitch of fitness. Given another fortnight or so, we felt confident that we should be ready for any task, however arduous, that might lie ahead.

Then, with the shock of a major disaster, the blow fell: we were ordered to be ready to leave in 48 hours time.

As usual not a single clue was given us; our destination might have been anywhere from Petsamo to the Black Sea. But even without any hints to go on, we had a feeling that something had misfired and that the 'party' was off. Pessimism spread like wildfire, a less pleasant accompaniment this time to the inevitable epidemic of speculation. Not that we minded quitting the Alps to tackle more serious business; what we did fear was something different – the fate of being disbanded.

The following morning, feeling rather like schoolboys being given a special treat, we were whisked off to the Col de Voza. This pass of 5,424 feet overlooks the valley several miles below Chamonix and is comfortably reached by bus and *téléphérique* (cable car). We found its broad, gently curved back undisturbed by the faintest trace of wind and in a few moments, as we moved off on our skis, we were feeling luxuriously warm in the sunshine. Under such perfect conditions gloomy thoughts about the future were impossible; enjoyment of the present was all that mattered. For several hours we swooped and swung over the dazzling hummocks of the ridge or down into the beautifully moulded punch bowls on either side, seizing greedily the maximum of delight from every valuable minute. There was novelty too in the views on this west side of Mont Blanc, and I wished more than ever for a large-scale map to explain the complex pattern of peaks and valleys.

Sunday, brilliant as ever with sunshine, brought an afternoon of leisure and a great climax to our week. A large party of us, with a few francs still to burn, decided to visit the Brévent, the 8,285-foot summit which overlooks Chamonix on the north and makes one of the finest 'popular' viewpoints in the Alps. Luckily there was no need to moderate our Sunday dinners for this, as the climb can be made entirely by *téléphérique*. The latter starts off soberly enough, but on its second 'leg' the little car swings out on its span-wires to make a sensational mid-air crossing of the mountain face. It soars high above a wide corrie, ribbed with gaunt black buttresses of rock, and not until the very end of the journey is a haven reached in the face of the cliff opposite. From here a short stone staircase leads upwards to a broad balcony, ideal for an afternoon of laziness.

We looked across the valley to Mont Blanc, seemingly loftier and more majestic than ever, with its snowfields and cataracts of ice shimmering in the afternoon glare. Beyond Mont Maudit stretched the ranks of the *aiguilles*, each tower and spire familiar now in shape, but still annoyingly lacking precise identification. East yet again the Aiguille Verte soared to its finely tapered snow-tip high above the Mer de Glace, and as I studied its perfection of line and symmetry I automatically gave it pride of place, with the Matterhorn and the Weisshorn, among all the Alpine peaks I knew.

Although sightseeing was enough to content most of our party, a few of the bolder spirits had taken their skis with them to the top of the Brévent, and from the cabin of the *téléphérique* as we swung away over the corrie, we could make out several of them on their way down. The descent looked far from simple, and in the evening we were duly regaled with hair-raising tales of running above immense precipices and desperate turns on sharp, icy bends. The honour of those who had so suffered the indignity of the nursery slopes was satisfied at last.

So ended our stay in Chamonix. Next morning we were up at 4.30 and away as the dawn light was tinting the highest peaks. At St Gervais we changed trains, with the old familiar chaos and curses, and then all too soon we were back on the plains of France, watching the lower foothills of the Alps growing faint in the hazy distance.

Annemasse, Bellegarde, Bourg, Dijon – laboriously the long troop train of fourteen coaches and nine goods wagons trundled northwards. This time there was less hurry, less sense of urgency. It was as if the French railways, the War Office, even our own officers had lost interest in us. Next morning we were at Rouen enjoying rolls, fruit, chocolate and wine, and by midday, almost 30 hours after leaving Chamonix, we were back in Le Havre.

Looking back now to the final phase of the 5th Battalion's 'life', it makes rather a crazy pattern against the broader background of wartime events. Apparently on 2 March France had at last decided to give active help to Finland by sending 50,000 volunteers together with

100 bombers. To this contribution Britain had agreed to add 50 bombers, but, according to Mr Churchill, it was not until ten days later, on 12 March, that the British War Cabinet determined to revive the plans for actual military landings. These were to be at Narvik and Trondheim, to be followed at Stavanger and Bergen. The date of this decision is interesting, for by a coincidence it was on the same day that Finland accepted Russia's armistice terms. What was in fact going on behind the diplomatic scenes is successfully hidden from the ordinary onlooker, but it is difficult to understand how, in face of the impending armistice, the Cabinet's action at that late date could be taken for anything better than a rather pathetic gesture. Perhaps it was that and nothing more, for the whole question of help for Finland seems to have been tackled from first to last with a remarkable amount of uncertainty and indecision.

On 12 March, the day of the armistice, we were at Le Havre and it would have been reasonable to expect that we should proceed forthwith back to Bordon for disbandment. But no; the part we were playing in this bizarre comedy was still not quite finished. Our hopes were to be raised once again before being finally dashed.

A peaceful channel-crossing in the small hours of the morning brought us back to Southampton and the first mail for nearly a fortnight. Then into the train again for what we imagined would be the last of our many journeys. But we were wrong. We travelled north and when nightfall brought no new destination, the embers of our optimism flickered once more into life. North across the Border to waken to frost and sunshine at Dumfries, and then we were clanking into Glasgow's King George V Dock, noisily astir with every sign of military embarkation. We even got the length of joining other units of a specially equipped division on board the troopship *Batory*. But the jubilation this aroused was fated to be short-lived. During the course of the day loading stopped and we saw only too plainly in the idle cranes the end of all our hopes. Next day we were marched down the gangway again and this time we knew for certain that we could only be Bordon-bound.

And so, back at Quebec Barracks we found ourselves mustered in the gym for a second dose of speech-making. There was not much doubt about the mood the battalion was in – the mood of a belligerent, angry mob. Cheer leaders climbed to positions of vantage and goaded us to more and more uproarious bellowings of our latest theme-song, *We won't be disbanded*. At signals from them we were to let rip and drown the General's remarks. The atmosphere grew tense as we waited, impatience adding fuel to our fury.

Then came anti-climax. Military police arrived and herded us outside the building. For half-an-hour we had to cool our heels in the fresh air. When finally the General did arrive and make his fateful pronouncement, not a murmur of protest was raised. In a few moments the 5th Battalion had ceased to exist.

We wandered off disconsolately to hand in our kit. Then in due course we went our several ways. A month later British troops were fighting in Norway. But, to quote Mr Churchill, 'They lacked aircraft, anti-aircraft guns, tanks, transport and training. The whole of Northern Norway was covered with snow to depths which none of our soldiers had ever seen, felt or imagined. There were neither snowshoes, nor skis – still less skiers. We must do our best. Thus began this ramshackle campaign.' Perhaps it is not altogether idle to speculate on the part that might have been played by the 5th Battalion had its existence been continued.

*****

Postscript: Some years after the war I happened to meet a former Scots Guards officer. Hoping, all innocent-like, to start a good conversation with him, I remarked that I too had been in the Scots Guards.

'Oh, really?' he queried. 'Which battalion was that?'

'The 5th,' I replied.

'The 5th? The 5th? No such battalion.'

And I was left to regret, not a little sadly, that my documentary War Office evidence was not available in my pocket, but lying at home firmly pasted into an old, half-forgotten album of wartime memorabilia.

Chapter Eight

ICELAND – 1940

IN early April 1940, less than three weeks after our Chamonix anti-climax, Germany was over-running Norway. Just how useful the 5th Battalion would have been in that bitter campaign is, I fear, a question with a very short answer. Yet at the time, for us who might well have been involved, the whole Scots Guards episode seemed as frustrating as it was clearly wasteful.

Knowing next to nothing about Norway, I bought a copy of Hugo's *Norwegian in Three Months*. This enabled me, rather to my own surprise, to make a back door entry into a Scandinavian-speaking Field Security section of the Intelligence Corps. The outcome, however, was not quite as expected: the unit was sent, not to Norway, but to Liverpool and thence nearly three months later – after Dunkirk and just as Britain was bracing itself to repel the invaders – to Iceland. It seemed distressingly like ignominious departure from the heat of battle.

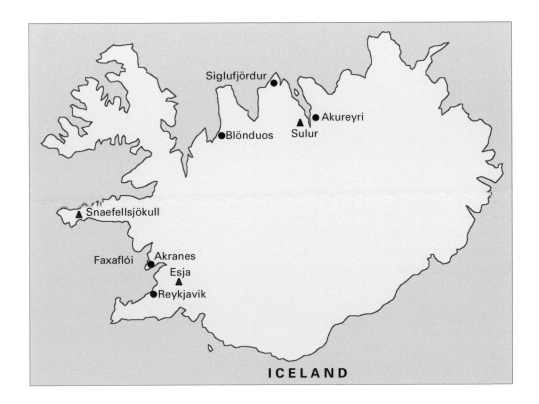

ICELAND

I suppose I knew just as much – or as little – about Iceland as my neighbour. It had been featured fairly prominently in the newspapers when, along with the Faeroes, it had been occupied by the British in order to forestall a German takeover. But in the hectic days of that fateful summer of 1940 the focus of interest kept changing so rapidly that the event had soon been forgotten. I knew of course that Iceland had a capital called Reykjavik and, for no obvious reason, a volcano called Hekla; also that Arctic explorers were wont to pause there before pushing on to the greater attractions of Greenland and even the Pole itself. But apart from that my knowledge was limited to vague memories of Loti's *Pêcheur d'Islande* and his graphic descriptions of the immensity and solitude of the fog-bound northern seas. In normal circumstances my enthusiasm would have been boundless. But these were times just about as abnormal as they could have been, so that my feelings when I came to meditate on our fate were thoroughly mixed.

We travelled north to Gourock and sailed in the *Georgic* from the Tail of the Bank on 28 July, moving off so gently in the small hours of the morning that I was blissfully unaware of the quickening pulse of the engines. Breakfast-time saw us steaming up the North Channel between Rathlin Isle and Kintyre and in mid-afternoon we had our last glimpse of Britain – the distant razor-edge of St Kilda. It was to be another 22 years before I saw St Kilda again, and a further eight before I was able to set foot on Hirta and climb Oiseval for the classic overhead view of Village Bay. Meanwhile, for the next 40 hours, we saw only the Atlantic, icy grey, cold and cheerless.

Although in those days I had to gaze from afar upon that obvious corner of paradise, the officers' quarters, there was nothing actually purgatorial in our own lot on the *Georgic*. I remember revelling in the novel luxury of hot salt baths between spells on deck watching the manoeuvres of our distant destroyer escort. I started to plan too, and even tried to bring reality into this by consulting the section's maps. These came to light as a most impressive roll – memory suggests bound with equally impressive red tape – and as I spread them out I could not help marvelling at the War Office's astuteness in having been prepared even for Iceland. Then I found the answer: they were a series of sheets designed for the use of the BEF – in France.

Iceland's welcome was unmistakably frigid. A broken coastline, slowly resolving itself into a succession of capes and cliffs and low, mist-draped peaks, had the depressing look of a lost world. Its grey monotony fitted all too subtly into the North Atlantic scene, of which we mere soldiers had already had more than enough. It was not until late in the morning that the sun condescended to take a hand, struggling through to dispel the clouds and some of the gloom, and by the time the *Georgic* had turned into the inner recesses of Reykjavik Bay, the day was actually acquiring quite a kindly warmth.

Reykjavik Bay, broad and spacious, is in some ways reminiscent of the Western Highlands. Its bordering carpet of moorland, too vast to be affected by the straggling, untidy city, stretches away southwards to a dim line of hills. Eastwards the shore is overlooked by the plateau of Esja, its flat table-top everywhere about 2,800 feet high and its flanks scarred by grey scree gullies. It reminded me faintly of Quinag, but without the curves of peak and buttress which give the Sutherland hill its character. Further round to the north and resting as vaguely as a cloud on the horizon, the white ice-cap of Snaefellsjökull showed up clearly. This was the first of the permanent snowfields I was to see in Iceland, and the glimpses I had of it, far off and indistinct though they were, seemed as tantalising as had been those of the Chamonix *aiguilles*. As in Scotland, all these views vary enormously with the visibility. One day sunshine may allow a true assessment of colour and distance; the next a smirr of rain may shut out the background with the finality of a theatre curtain.

Our first trip ashore was on a day of low clouds and slanting rain when sightseeing was a doubtful pleasure. Perhaps we should have seen more than just grey masonry in the exterior of the historic Althing building, or admired the modernistic lines of the black stuccoed National Theatre, but I must confess that, from the first, Reykjavik's chief virtue seemed to be as a jumping-off place.

Our second visit, brightened by sun-blinks, was more pleasing. Fortified by the belief that our Icelandic was making dazzling progress, we achieved a lunch of rhubarb soup, salted mutton and coffee at a cost of roughly two shillings. The meal was served by a waitress in national costume – black dress with gold embroidery and a form of skull cap with black tassel – said to be of Norwegian origin. Of more recent inspiration was a notice in English which we saw afterwards prominently displayed in a shop window: 'Fish and Chips. At Times.'

In the afternoon we chartered a taxi and motored out some 10 miles to the small village and subsidiary port of Hafnarfjördur. Our driver was an enthusiastic guide and kept up a running commentary in a bewildering mixture of Icelandic and Danish. It was impossible to be even moderately polite when one had only the haziest idea whether he was describing the British 'invasion', the eruptions of Hekla, or merely the curing of fish. However, he evidently mistook our vacant expressions for intelligence, for his ardour remained undimmed.

Much to our delight we learned that our further destination was the North Coast. The prospect was compensation even for our transfer to the *Koningin Emma*, quite the worst troopship it has ever been my misfortune to set foot on. A Dutch cross-channel steamer normally on the Harwich–Flushing service, it had nothing, not even good looks, to commend it. It had rolled westwards across the Atlantic in company with the *Georgic* and we had often felt sorry for the luckless troops on board; had we known then what we found out later, our sympathy would have been still greater. Probably the worst of our troubles was the lack of a canteen, for an unvarying diet of army biscuits, margarine and tea can lose its appeal with quite remarkable speed.

We steamed out into the evening sunshine on a day of clear skies and long views, and as we headed northwards across the huge coastal indent of Faxaflói in the wake of our escorting trawler, only a slow, lazy swell came rolling in from the Atlantic. I was impatient for the first near views of Snaefellsjökull, the 4,744- foot glaciated volcano we had already seen on the horizon, but I had underestimated its distance from Reykjavik – some 70 miles – and as the hours passed we seemed to draw no closer. I decided therefore to spend the night on deck and carried blankets and greatcoat to a sheltered cranny under the corner of a tarpaulin. The idea was excellent, but I had reckoned without the weather: even although it was light all night, at 2am, just when we were at last in position, a mist-screen was down well below the rim of the crater. Beyond, for hour after hour, we looked shorewards across an inhospitable waste of water to scenery that changed little in detail. Above a thin line of surf and hostile defences of reefs and stacks, the hills beyond were flat-topped, as though their upper cones had been sliced off by some giant knife. Undramatically we rounded the 'Horn', the north-west jut of Iceland, and crossed the Arctic Circle.

The *Koningin Emma* docked at Akureyri at four o'clock in the morning – some 32 hours after leaving Reykjavik – at which point, like the Fat Boy at the Pickwickian rook-shooting, I was 'more than three parts and a fraction asleep.' Situated some two miles from the head of the 30-mile-long Eyjafjördur, 'fjord of the isles', Akureyri is a picturesque little place, at that time with about 6,000 inhabitants. Its houses rise steeply behind the harbour, with the modern church prominent in the centre. Opposite, on the eastern side of the fjord, a level ridge dotted here and there with white farm buildings runs southwards to the wide glens of the hinterland. Above the town itself the background is on a grander scale – higher, snow-streaked peaks and, showing through a gap, a magnificent wedge of glacier with an imposing eastern face.

The weather seemed to have taken a turn for the better, the dry, dusty roads indicating a recent hot spell, so that I was glad when the opportunity occurred next day for an assault on Súlur (3,753ft), the 'pillar', the nearest prominent peak. Actually it was not till almost 6pm that my companion and I were able to set out, but with the long summer evening before us, we clearly had plenty of time.

The road climbed steeply out of the town to an expanse of moorland, tilting tediously upwards to the first shoulder. Thereafter, before the final screes, a long, flat saddle had to be crossed, made doubly desolate, as I well remember, by the piping of numerous golden plover, no doubt finished with their nesting and soon to be off southwards on their autumn journeying to Britain. A drifting curtain of mist hid some of the views, but eastwards ridge upon ridge of rolling hills, not unlike the Cairngorms, were aglow in the evening light, while Eyjafjördur to the north seemed to flow like a golden river to the sea.

Sadly there was no sequel on the Akureyri hills. With only a couple of days' breathing space, three of us were sent off on detachment to Siglufjördur, some 35 miles nearer the North Pole. We left at eight o'clock in the morning in rather doubtful weather on board the little milk-boat *Mjölnir*, and it was not until after four in the afternoon that we reached our

One of the Icelandic herring fleet at Siglufjördur.

destination. Our progress throughout was of that amiable, leisurely kind, reminiscent of a journey to Mallaig on the West Highland railway. Sometimes we stopped for some good reason such as changing passengers or cargo, and sometimes we just stopped. We even managed a break for coffee and cakes on the island of Hrisey, near the mouth of Eyjafjördur, and as if this was not enough to keep us from boredom, the skipper entertained us in the wheelhouse with an enormous bottle of milk, while the deck boy played his accordion and sang. Even the weather seemed determined to do its bit, clearing up as we turned westwards along the open coast. This was particularly welcome, for some of the scenery was remarkably fine, stupendous rock walls, hundreds of feet high, rising tier upon tier, ledge upon ledge, to torn and splintered crests. It was not until we had chugged round the point of Siglunes to within three miles of our destination that we could rediscover any signs of friendliness in our surroundings.

Siglutjördur, where I was destined to spend the next 10 weeks, lies on the west side of the fjord of the same name. In 1940 it was the great herring fishing centre of Iceland, presenting a scene of ceaseless, bustling activity. To its forty-odd quays of varying size, age and decrepitude the deeply laden herring boats kept chugging monotonously in, day and night, from the open sea. Its five factories, from which emanated an all-pervasive smell, raced against a remorseless time schedule as the stores of oil and meal steadily increased, the hands working two shifts of six hours every day with only one shift off each week. Deeply involved was the army of girls, gutting, cleaning, packing, seemingly without rest. Everyone, indeed, in his or her own way was bound up with the all-important, inescapable *síld* (herring). It was only with the coming of autumn – as we discovered in due course –

that this feverish tempo slackened. Unobtrusively the boats disappeared to their winter havens; the hundreds of workers, richer perhaps but dog-weary too, departed to Reykjavik or the Westmann Islands, and the town resigned itself to slipping quietly into another spell of hibernation.

Yet today, I'm told, all that is changed. The story is very different. The herring have gone and the factories, presumably, have closed. Siglufjördur is now no more than a ghost town.

Enclosing the fjord is a deep horseshoe of hills, steep-sided with here and there steps of bare rock. The barrier indeed is so complete that in those wartime days there was no access to the town by road, unless one counted the pony-track crossing a high pass to the west. Otherwise sea and air provided the only connections with the outside world.

This last feature had some bearing on our Army duties, which certainly could not have been described as arduous. In the main they consisted of looking out for any suspiciously pro-German behaviour, noting in particular the arrival or movements of any unusual characters. However, with no exit to the country's interior, Siglufjördur seemed an improbable choice as a spy-ring hub, while the thought of its being selected as a site for invasion gave us cause for few sleepless nights.

It did not take us long to settle down to life in the town. Two of us found billets with a Dane and his Icelandic wife, and we could not possibly have received greater kindness. Hailing originally from Copenhagen, Erik was a civil engineer and at that time was busy with the town's latest developments in harbour construction. Much more important from our point of view was the fact that he was one of the best natural humorists I have ever known. Whether in good Danish, moderate Icelandic or atrocious English, his sense of fun was enormous and conversation with him usually became as boisterous as a Christmas pantomime. Although we had our meals out, we had a standing invitation to look in for coffee in the evenings and this we did gladly as often as we could, usually chatting till long after midnight. Nor did late hours matter unduly, for our coffee and cake breakfasts were brought up to us in our room, where we reclined in state upon divan beds. I could never quite bring myself to ask for a hot water bottle or put my boots out for polishing; never shall it be said that the honour of the British Army was sullied, however much it was in jeopardy.

Although our meals out tended to be decidedly monotonous, there were the occasional notable exceptions. One such, I remember, began with rhubarb soup – other varieties we encountered were prune, raisin and apricot – and continued with lavish helpings of smoked mutton. Finally we were confronted by two large bowls, one containing blaeberries and the other *skyr*. This latter is a favourite Icelandic dish, being clotted sour milk that looks like whipped cream but has in fact a rather firmer consistency. It is sold in the local dairies and borne home usually in the morning paper, much as one might carry off a portion of fish and chips. I personally found it tasty enough – in moderation.

Siglufjördur was no different from any other town the world over in its desire to

Systirnir, 'the Sisters', two peaks above Siglufjördur, northern Iceland.

provide entertainment, and to some extent it succeeded. There was, for example, the cinema. This was nothing more than a converted hall, with stone floor and austerity benches which made it as cold and cheerless as a prison. Films were almost all of British or American origin, with Danish subtitles – a very necessary aid since the sound reproduction was unintelligible. There were two performances every day, each consisting of one full-length film, without trimmings such as newsreels or shorts, and programmes were changed daily. Whenever the stock was exhausted, the series was simply started again, so that, if so minded, one could see old favourites such as *Robin Hood* approximately once every three weeks. One evening I was misguided enough to attend a showing of *Pygmalion*. It was unbelievably bad. Not a titter did it raise from the audience and only the most dour determination to get my money's worth gave me strength to sit it through to the end.

Much more entertaining was the nightly dancing at the local hotel. This might aptly be put under the heading of 'Blood Sports'. Regularly dancefloor and tables were packed beyond capacity with a hot and noisy throng of fishermen, herring girls, worthies of the town and a few British soldiers. Comparatively safe in a corner, the local quartet blared out their cacophony of threadbare numbers, of which the hottest were *Roll out the Barrel* and *Oh, Johnny, how you can love!* A good time for all was assured. Suddenly there would be a crash. For no obvious reason a table would be pushed over, or a bottle would fly. The fun had started. Usually it was a momentary flare-up, a quick squall that passed and was soon forgotten, though sometimes the melee became general, sweeping dancers and onlookers alike into its boisterous eddies. Backwards and forwards the tide would surge, but as even the chief participants rarely knew what all the trouble was about, everything remained remarkably good-humoured and friendly. It was only on the very special occasions when the local constabulary intervened that matters looked serious. They looked so frail! It was clear from the start that they would go under and go under they invariably did, for the combatants, as Para Handy remarked of the Tarbert fishermen, 'didna have aromatic pistols, but they had aawfully aromatic fists.' The only hope was help from the two British military policemen. One had been a Scots Guardsman and the other a heavyweight boxer good enough to fight the pre-war German champion Walter Neusel. Before their majestic advance the tumult would subside and order re-emerge from chaos. In a moment, as if nothing at all untoward had happened, the dancing would be in full swing once again.

Round the head of the fjord the horseshoe barrier of hills was ideal for ridge-wandering. Quickly accessible from the town and reaching for the most part between 2,500 and 3,000 feet, the switchback was particularly suitable for solitary evening sorties. I escaped there as often as I could, finding even a modest few miles alone a real antidote to the jostle and noise of the town's nightlife. Usually in the earlier days the sun would be setting, glowing red against a mother-of-pearl background of sky and sea, finally dipping and vanishing somewhere beyond Greenland and the Arctic ice. As if to stress the loneliness, the pencil island outline of Grimsey was silhouetted a darker grey almost 40 miles away on the north-eastern horizon, in imagination the ultimate piece of land before the Pole.

Once, up on the ridge at the beginning of autumn, I was treated to a spectacular show of the northern lights. At first I mistook them for thin films of cloud, but their display grew so rapidly in extent and beauty that I was unable to avert my gaze even at the risk of a broken neck. Causeways of silver, vast arches of white, curtains and streamers of green and purple formed a broad and flickering canopy over the zenith. And all in almost uncanny silence. It was the most wonderful show of the aurora I had ever seen and the magnificence of it held me spellbound. Then the moon came up, more homely indeed, yet in its way scarcely less striking with its reflections in the quiet fjord at my feet. For the first time I felt I was really being privileged to know something of the true meaning of the Arctic night.

As the October days passed, there was a real foretaste of winter: the first snows deepened on the hills and even a fringe of ice edged the shallows of the fjord. Now, with much earlier darkness and without proper boots or other equipment, the chances to enjoy ridge-walks were few.

One outing I did enjoy before there was too much snow was to the higher of the twin-peaked Systirnir, the 'Sisters', the most attractive of all the surrounding summits. The two tops rise sharply from the eastern shore of the fjord and are united by a graceful sickle of ridge, itself the wall of a deep and shadowed corrie. Unfortunately the only available day I had was one of venomous wind, a gale that blasted and bullied me all the way round the corrie lip. Some of the gusts were so violent that they whipped scree-dust and even small stones from some of the ledges, while the more tottery rock towers looked liable to disintegrate before the onslaught. Nevertheless it was all immensely satisfying, a real day to remember in thinking back to that remote horseshoe of hills through the shifting mists of the years.

ICELAND – 1940

A posting back to the UK in mid-October meant farewell not just to Siglufjördur but to Iceland itself – sadly there has been no return. I left in the milk-boat early on a morning of biting frost. Eastwards along the coast, we came again under the great sea-cliffs, white-rimmed now in places with snow cornices, blackly forbidding lower down where no sun reached them. Now and again we passed a swaying fishing smack, lending touches of contrast by its movement. But the hours passed slowly and even when eventually we swung south into Eyjafjördur, many miles still lay ahead. By the time we were approaching Akureyri the shadows were lengthening in the early gloaming.

For the next stage of the journey one main road – an Icelandic motorway of the day – spanned a vast corner of the island from Akureyri in the north to Akranes, a distance of more than 250 miles. It was southwards over this road that I was to travel the following day, completing the last stage from Akranes to Reykjavik by ferry across an inlet of the huge bay of Faxaflói.

I set off at seven o'clock. It was still dark and bitterly cold as the long-distance bus, a roomy 16-seater Chevrolet, bumped out of the town, mist muffling the early morning sounds. The surface of the road proved to be anything but of motorway standard and the prospect of a long, uncomfortable day was not especially pleasing. Already we felt stiff enough as we climbed out for breakfast at an isolated inn 30 miles on our way. A thermometer at the door, I noticed, was registering one and a half degrees Centigrade: after our meal we escaped from the low-lying cloud, but the scenery, though sunlit, remained hour after hour uniformly monotonous. All the way across the island it scarcely varied – bleak, dun-coloured moorland, with here and there a twisting, rather lethargic river and a background of featureless hills. Even the sole village, Blönduós by name, where we lunched and where we had our last glimpse of the north coast, was not as big as Crianlarich. Certainly we saw lonely farmsteads now and again and in the valleys numerous Icelandic ponies were grazing, but otherwise desolation characterised the landscape on every side.

About five o'clock in the afternoon we entered the lava country and I saw again those rolling hillsides, bristling with tortured, twisted rocks. For a little while the twilight lingered over this weird lost world, then darkness fell and for the last few miles to Akranes there was nothing to see but the swinging beams of the headlights. We were not sorry to transfer at last from the jolting, swaying bus to the ferry, which carried us across to Reykjavik and that part of journey's end. That night my bed on an accommodating sergeant-major's floor seemed as soft as down.

There were two final days in the capital, one, not surprisingly, wet. The other was frosty and bright enough to allow a companion and myself to circle the bay on motorbikes and climb Esja (2,795ft) – mostly a stroll up grassy moorland and scree to a tableland top, with far views to the south-east, an unbroken line of white, probably Hekla's neighbours.

Then, early on 29 October, I was ferried out to the *Empress of Australia*, which, along with the Cunard White Star Line troopship *Antonia*, was carrying a large number of

Canadians to Britain. Forty-eight hours later we drew slowly out of Reykjavik Bay behind the armed merchantman which was to be our escort. It was another bleak morning, with a light curtain of rain, and soon, as we gathered speed, Reykjavik grew indistinct against its moorland background. Gradually Iceland itself became no more than a vague, indefinite coastline, finally swallowed up in the grey of sky and sea.

My fellow travellers, the Canadians, were in high spirits. Most of them belonged to the Royal Regiment and were looking forward to their first visit to Britain. Sparkling conversation and lusty singing came easily to them, and I never stopped marvelling at the candour of their patriotism or the way they would chorus *Tipperary* and *Pack up your Troubles* as though these songs were completely new and unworn.

Now, more than 60 years on and with the hindsight of history, it is profoundly sobering to reflect on how so easily that carefree chorusing might have been silenced, how but for the timing of Providence our own feebly protected convoy might well have been annihilated.

It was on 31 October that we left Reykjavik. Just four days earlier the newly com- missioned German pocket-battleship *Scheer* had broken out into the Atlantic through the Denmark Strait north of Iceland. Under orders to attack North Atlantic convoys, she was already steaming south to wreak havoc among a convoy of 37 ships eastward-bound like ourselves which had just left Halifax, Nova Scotia. Escorting the convoy was the armed merchant cruiser *Jervis Bay*, commanded by Captain Fegen, RN.

Faced with hopeless odds, Captain Fegen endeavoured to engage the pocket-battleship for as long as possible to allow the convoy to disperse under cover of darkness. But the task was impossible. His ship, heavily on fire and out of control, went down with the loss of 200 officers and men; of the convoy, in all 47,000 tons of shipping and 206 merchant seamen were lost. A posthumous award of the Victoria Cross was made to Captain Fegen for his gallantry.

All unaware of this desperate battle so near us, we settled to enjoy our own placid voyage. On the second day out there was real artistry in the seascape, with the sky a patchwork of pale blue, white and grey, while the waves, tipped with foam, had lost their sullenness in the sunshine. Our small convoy, zig-zagging endlessly, completed the picture, into which the gulls and, once, a rainbow fitted naturally. By midday the wind had freshened though the sun shone more brightly, and great bursts of spray whitened the bows of the ships. Next morning when I emerged on deck I was delighted to find that the coast of Scotland was in sight. To the east, under a turreted cloud-bank red-rimmed by the dawn, stood the ranks of the Sutherland hills – Quinag, Canisp, Suilven, Stac Polly, Ben More Coigach. 'Looks like we're back in Iceland again,' complained the Canadians. But I did not echo their sentiments. These hills, after all, were old friends and as such were according me a generous welcome home.

Chapter Nine

LOCHAILORT TO
LAND'S END – 1943-1945

THE Iceland interlude was followed by one or two interesting postings – interesting, yes, but almost completely chairborne. And these were restless days. So, when the chance came to go on a fieldcraft course at Lochailort, I seized it eagerly with both hands.

Tucked away at the head of a right-angled sea inlet, the village cluster of Lochailort is the next stop after Glenfinnan on the West Highland railway, roughly two-thirds of the way from Fort William to Mallaig. The surrounding terrain, isolated, rugged, adequately wooded, is ideal for outdoor training days – and nights – especially in early summer before the massed onslaught of the midges.

About the course itself there was nothing humdrum; it was as varied as it was strenuous. Speed-marching, bivouacking, unarmed (not noticeably gentle) combat, recipes for survival – it was all a memorable mixture. The instructors too were impressive: among them Admiral Murray Levick, who had been with Scott in the Antarctic, extolling the food-virtue of gulls' eggs and berries; those legendary masters of in-fighting, Fairbairn and Sykes, on loan, I would guess, from the Commando Basic Training Centre at Achnacarry; expert in lightweight travel, J.M. Scott, formerly sledging partner of Gino Watkins in Greenland.

Also there, but working on his own, was fellow-member of the Scottish Mountaineering Club Sandy Wedderburn (who, sadly, when second-in-command of the Lovat Scouts was later in the war to lose his life in Italy). Following service with the Scots Guards ski battalion, Sandy had been very much involved in Combined Operations training in Iceland and the US as well as at home in Britain. At Lochailort he was particularly busy trying to persuade the War Office that the British Army was in urgent need of a sizeable proportion of mountain troops in its make-up. While France had the Chasseurs Alpins, Germany its Bergtruppen and Italy the Alpini – troops which could fight as effectively in the mountains as in lowland country – Britain had none. The lessons of Norway needed to be learned – and soon.

The results of Sandy's efforts were neither large-scale nor dramatic, yet along with seeds sown by others they helped to bear fruit in both the short and long term.

A development in December 1942 was the formation of the Commando Mountain

Warfare Training Centre (CMWTC), initially to train commando troops to fight in high snow-covered mountain country. The unit's first base for this was at Braemar, allowing six months of hard winter training in the Cairngorms in which Nos 1, 4 and 12 Commandos took part. The decision was then taken, however, not to use commando troops specifically in this role and the unit was moved to North Wales to train the Lovat Scouts as a mountaineer battalion.

After Lochailort, where several commando officers had been among those taking part, I was reluctant to revert once again to tamer duty. However, it was not until late September 1943 that opportunity knocked again: I was given the chance of going to Wales as one of the instructors at the CMWTC.

My only previous acquaintance with the mountains of Snowdonia had been, as described earlier, a brief weekend of planned enjoyment and unplanned discomfort. Sometimes, in the autumn of 1943, the weather pattern seemed like a copycat version of that night of misery experienced at Pen-y-Gwryd. Certainly I have always maintained that for our three months in Wales it rained, hailed or sleeted every single day. An exaggeration maybe, yet not far wide of the mark. No doubt it was good for toughening us up, but it would have been pleasure indeed to work now and again on warm, dry rocks, or to have just a few far, clear views from the summit of Snowdon.

The Lovats, who were newly back from a spell of 'guard duty' in the Faeroes, included many stalkers and keepers, hillmen born and bred, so it seemed altogether presumptuous to think that we could give them many hints on mountaincraft. There was novelty for them all the same in the actual rock-climbing and they were obviously keen to gain experience.

One aspect of the training was a constant strong emphasis on safety. This was outstandingly well observed by Major Geoffrey Rees Jones, who at the time of the move south from Braemar had taken over as commanding officer from Squadron Leader Frank Smythe, the well-known Everest climber of pre-war days. Geoffrey never let up the whole time he was in command; instructors and trainees alike were well advised to heed an eagle eye that missed precisely nothing.

Thanks largely to this there was not a single fatality during our autumn in Wales. There was, however, one accident which did occur and which might well have ruined the record – Lieut. Maurice Drummond of the Lovats fell while leading a climb on the Facet of the Gribin, one morning of sleet and greasy rock. The result of his fall was a fractured skull and a long ambulance ride to hospital. Thereafter we knew nothing of how things had fared with Maurice, only that his mishap had not been fatal. The answer in fact – with happy ending – did not come to our knowledge until 40 years later. Not long after we had come to live in Perthshire we went to visit the Scottish Wildlife Trust centre at the Loch of the Lowes, near Dunkeld. To my very great surprise and delight we were greeted by the warden

High-speed abseil practice, Tryfan, North Wales.

***

– Maurice Drummond himself. And he was as cheery as ever I had known him, fit and exuberantly well.

Of the actual climbs we did I have no clear recollection, only that they were many and varied – linking the ample ledges of Tryfan, moving round to the slabs of Idwal, going further afield to Lliwedd, or solving the more assorted problems of the Glyders. Sometimes, too, when the weather was so hostile that one actually had to admit to loathing the touch of naked rock, there would be practice at lower levels on less wind-whipped crags. And whatever the day, rain, hail or shine, training invariably ended with an obligatory half hour of abseiling. The technique used was the Geneva, or *rappel à la genevoise*, and this allowed such fiercely high speeds to be reached, that we came to feel we could almost take off down the crags without the encumbrance of a rope.

In between whiles there were occasional cross-country exercises, at which, of course, the Lovats excelled. One such expedition provided the grand finale to our time in Snowdonia. A long day on the Carnedds in the usual mist and rain, carrying arms and equipment, brought us to Ogwen and the concession of a shortish rest. Thereafter a crossing in the dark and still unrelenting rain took us over to Pen-y-Pass, in turn the prelude to a dawn attack on the summit of Snowdon. As observers of this final assault, we had to start up Snowdon at 3am or thereabouts – a doubtful pleasure after a decidedly moist 'sleep' outstretched on a bench in a Pen-y-Pass barn. Of the success or otherwise of the assault I have no recollection whatever; all I do remember is, after it was all over, cantering full tilt down the 'Pyg Track' to a mighty breakfast at Pen-y-Pass.

In December 1943 our Army unit was split three ways. The Lovats went out to Canada for snow – more particularly ski – training in the Rockies; a number of those who had been instructing in Wales went with them and on thereafter to bitter fighting in Italy. Several others were posted to a mountaineering school in Lebanon. The remaining third, of which I was a member, moved to St Ives, in Cornwall, away from the December rain and sleet to Mediterranean-like mildness, to palm trees and even to Christmas bathing. There were other duties in store.

St Ives in wartime was an altogether ideal base, especially for those unacquainted with Cornwall. Coastal resorts were out of bounds to visitors, so that beaches and cobbled streets alike were quietly, picturesquely uncrowded. Nor did it take long for those in authority over us to decide that Cornish cream and lobsters were as good excuses as any for coming down on visits of inspection.

The main reason for our move to Cornwall was that in the original plan for D-Day two of the then new Marine Commandos were to assault the Normandy coast by way of cliffs rather than by the beaches, each led in by half of our St Ives unit. Consequently the troops of Nos 46 and 45 RM Commandos came for training, followed by troops of No.47, which were to be held in reserve. The words 'Mountain Warfare' in our unit's title, now little more than a standing joke, were retained as a deceptive measure. Preparations were made with the greatest thoroughness. We learned from aerial photographs how to assess the sea-cliff difficulties likely to be met with and we even experimented with the most unsporting methods – for example the use of cunningly designed grapnels, rocket propelled, and even firemen's ladders wheeled in to the cliff base.

In the event this planning went for nothing: the two clifftop batteries which it was intended should be silenced on D-Day by the marines had already been put out of action by the RAF and landings were made by way of the beaches after all. Of the St Ives contingent Captain Norman Easton (later Major) and Sergeant (later Captain) Joe Barry went ashore and fought with 46 Commando till D plus 50 and again later for a further spell, Norman winning the MC at the crossing of the Elbe.

For most of the team of instructors at St Ives sea-cliff climbing was a completely new experience. For one thing a walk downhill to the start of the day's climbing was an agreeable exchange for a more usual uphill moorland slog. Of more significance, however, was the heightened sense of exposure experienced when climbing above surf. This was something one became used to fairly quickly, but it had to be remembered, especially on days of wild wind and waves, as a definite added worry for any trainees just beginning to get the feel of the rocks.

Since the war the Cornish cliffs have become a highly popular climbing playground with a wealth of documented routes. When we were working there, however, the descriptions we had were scanty to say the least and out of date; mostly we had to work things out for ourselves. In any event choice of areas and routes had to relate more to training needs than to personal preferences.

There was immense variety all along the coast, from nearby Gurnards Head, past Porthmoina Cove and down to the harder routes of Sennen, then right round Land's End to the short climbs and 'bouldering' of Porthgwarra and Porthcurno. Well beyond were Cadgwith and Kynance near the Lizard (with the temptation of a Cornish tearoom in Penzance to resist in the bygoing). Well remembered also are the rugged granite ridge of Carn les Boel, one tip of the big Mill Bay sickle, and the amiable twin buttresses of Land's End itself, where on a warm day one could bask on some sun-trap ledge and let the gaze wander over the Atlantic blue to the skerries and lighthouse of the Longships, or further still to the slender pencil of the Wolf Rock.

By far the most important – and indeed enjoyable – training route was the Bosigran Ridge, one of the spectacular boundary edges of Porthmoina Cove, some eight miles along the coast from St Ives. From the very first it came to play an outstanding part in the ongoing work of the unit. It became a familiar, much-frequented highway both by day and by night, so that it was particularly fitting when, after the war, in the summer of 1946, a commemorative plaque was affixed to it, ensuring for all time its official name of 'Commando Ridge'.

It was Norman Easton who introduced me to the Ridge. He and I had previously climbed together on a number of occasions, summer and winter, in both Scotland and Wales, though never before on a December morning so sunny that the rock was almost hot to the touch. He had come down to St Ives with one or two of the other instructors some days before me and had lost no time in sampling the best that Cornwall had to offer.

The start we chose was from a diminutive earthy platform, the curling surf below emphasising the feeling of being suspended in mid-air. From here the ridge arches up and back for several hundreds of feet, its blade narrowing at times to a handsbreadth, yet with holds so rough and reassuring that there are no really hard technical difficulties. On one side the slopes disappear into the undercut depths of the cove; on the other the ground falls away with equal steepness, so that an exhilarating sense of exposure is never lacking.

Norman, I remember, was in particularly exuberant mood, pausing every now and again to produce the tin whistle from which he could seldom be separated. Thereafter the thin strains of *The Road to the Isles* or some such air floated unmelodiously out over the hollow of the cove. Though we could not have guessed it then, that same whistle was to be heard by others months later, on the Normandy beaches, on the banks of the Maas and the Rhine, and, most notably, in the heat of battle at the Elbe.

After that first sunny day, there were more visits to the Ridge than I could count. There were fun climbs and climbs with full kit, night climbs and climbs to enliven the occasional visits of posses of top brass. While we were at St Ives it entered significantly into our way of life.

It was in Halldrine's Cove, next to Porthmoina, that my own personal antics came most nearly to a premature end. The climb in question was quite short and simple – a knight's move up to a roomy platform and from there a genial 40-foot chimney shaped like an open book. The trouble occurred during the approach to the platform, at a place where it was necessary to swing out on the hands alone, round a big granite block the size of a double pillar-box. The block looked solid enough. It also felt solid. But it wasn't, and when I was half way round, my feet treading thin air, it moved very slightly – but very ominously. Why it failed to come away completely I have never understood, for the few millimetres it gave seemed like a sickening lurch. I held my breath and inched gingerly to safety. Then, with little more than a finger-touch, I sent the offending two-ton block crashing to the boulder-floor below.

It was, however, not so much the rocks as the sea which presented the most serious danger. The ferocity of the breakers which batter the Cornish peninsula has to be seen to be believed, and we quickly learned that at any time of wild weather there was constant risk anywhere near the highest tide's fringe. Even with repeated warnings to keep what seemed almost ridiculously well clear, it was quite frighteningly easy to be deceived into straying within the grasp of the occasional monster roller. There was in fact one tragedy at the foot of the Land's End cliffs, when two American servicemen on leave were caught unawares by an outsize wave which hurled them from the rocks into the maelstrom of surf below. A girl

One of the fine granite ridges near Land's End used in climbing training.

who was with them was more fortunate, as she was swept upwards to a ledge high on the cliff and was later brought to safety by the coastguards.

We ourselves managed to avoid any disaster so serious, although one incident that occurred during a night exercise came perilously close to tragedy. An evil sea had been running all day, making it impossible to come ashore from small boats in the customary way and with the planned assault having to be carried out from an imaginary landing point at the foot of the cliffs. Seven men were awaiting their turn to make the climb, standing on a rock platform supposedly out of reach of the very hostile breakers. The CO and I had been watching from a higher vantage point, when suddenly we were horrified to observe out to sea a monster 'seventh' wave sweeping inexorably landwards. Realising what was certainly going to happen, we started down toward the platform, in my case, I remember, removing my wristwatch and stuffing it into a niche in the rocks, hopefully above high tide mark. In the semi-darkness we saw the men hit by the wave and tossed pell-mell into an insane welter of surf. Then, as we tried to see just what we could do to help, unbelievably they reappeared one after the other, materialising miraculously out of the gloom. All were drenched, bruised and very shaken, but without so much as a cracked bone. Providentially a trough in the rocks behind the platform had put a brake on the backwash, thus lessening the suction that otherwise would have been irresistible. It had been a close call, much too close for comfort. Despite a lengthy search next day, I never found my watch.

After the flurry of D-Day, training was centred less on climbing itself, much more on the use of small boats. For rocky, steep-to landings and high speed hit-and-run recces we had the co-operation of the Navy. They had to learn almost as much as we had about this art and to begin with it all smacked more than a little of Lewis Carroll:

> But the danger was past – they had landed at last,
>> With their boxes, portmanteaus, and bags:
> Yet at first sight the crew were not pleased with the view,
>> Which consisted of chasms and crags.

Our naval friends did actually manage to write off completely one of their small, LCP(L), landing craft among some particularly hostile cliff-base boulders, an achievement regarded with little favour in High Places. It was remarkable how speedily thereafter greater proficiency all round was achieved.

For ourselves, we had half a dozen 18-foot dories – useful craft, if temperamental as mules – and with these we practised long and hard close to St Ives itself. The sandy beaches of Porthminster and Carbis Bay provided excellent opportunities for every type of landing, day and night. The dory – and accompanying rubber dinghy – had already proved its worth on various Commando reconnaissance raids in both Normandy and the Middle East; now we were to carry on the tradition, developing little by little our own operational technique, confident that it would be suitably fault-free.

We wondered if the chance would be happening along that would allow theory to be put into actual operational practice. It did – more testingly than we bargained for – in mid-autumn, 1944.

Chapter Ten

WALCHEREN – 1944

Remembering
Lieutenant Syd Richardson
killed in action
1 November 1944

I N the autumn of 1944, after the heady impetus following the Normandy landings, the Allies had blasted their way through much of Belgium to face the crossing of the Scheldt and the opening up of Antwerp on their onward sweep to the Rhine.

The forward thrust on the Allied left flank was initially considered sufficiently important to merit the strongest possible support. Assurances were given at top level that airborne troops would be made available, along with a sustained concentration of heavy bombing. In the event these hopes were not realised: the terrain was considered unsuitable for parachute or glider landings and the bombers were diverted elsewhere, as priority was given to the drive towards the Ruhr and the German heartland. The offensive was left in the main to ground troops alone.

Two simultaneous thrusts in the advance were to be an assault from the sea on the

**WALCHEREN
1944**

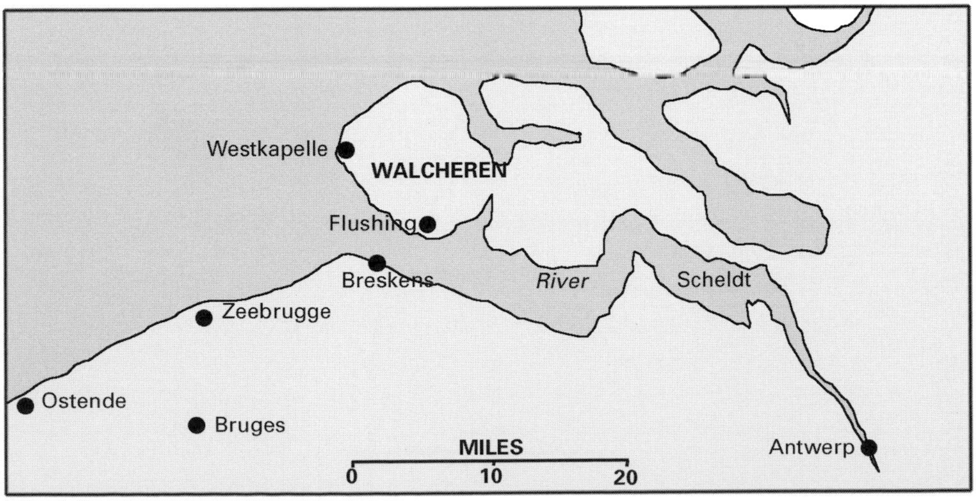

Westkapelle

WALCHEREN

Flushing

Breskens   *River*   Scheldt

Zeebrugge

Ostende

Bruges

Antwerp

MILES

0   10   20

Dutch island of Walcheren – along with the Hague one of the two remaining launching sites of V2 rockets within the operative 200-mile range of London – and a leap across the Scheldt estuary from Breskens to Flushing.

Walcheren is one of those saucer islands off the coast of the Netherlands with an interior below sea level, but reclaimed in typical Dutch fashion, with sea-wall and dyke in places 25 to 30 feet high and over 300 feet wide. As a prelude to the island being invaded the wall had earlier been bombed and breached at Westkapelle by the RAF, creating a 75-yard gap, so that the whole of the island's interior was deeply flooded. At the gap itself, where the assault from the sea was to be carried out, the tides were known to be particularly vicious, while the strength of the defending garrison was reported to be formidable.

In the preparations for D-Day several small-scale reconnaissance raids on the Normandy beaches had been carried out by the Commandos and these had been particularly successful. It was decided, therefore, that the Westkapelle gap and its immediate surroundings should be similarly reconnoitred prior to the sea assault there by No.4 Special Service Brigade. The task of carrying out the recces was allotted to our centre in Cornwall and a small unit was duly selected. Detailed to work with us were two Army signals personnel and four Marine Commando mine disposal experts. Overall command of the unit was given to Captain R.W. Keep from Commando Group headquarters.

So, on 6 October 'Keepforce', as we were called, duly travelled from Dover to Ostende, a stormy 10-hour crossing by minesweeper uncomfortably suggestive of the shape of things to come. In Ostende we joined up with the naval parent ship we were to be working with, *MTB No.621*, of 55 Flotilla, Coastal Forces, and her captain, Lt.Cdr. Whitby, RNVR.

The most important ingredient of these small-scale raids was the 18-foot dory, the type we had been practising with so assiduously in Cornwall. The operational pattern is that the MTB as the parent ship carries the dory, slung aft on davits, to approximately 1,000 yards offshore; the dory, with a complement of up to eight, is then launched and, towing a rubber dinghy, proceeds to 100 yards or so from the beach. Thereafter the dinghy, with up to five aboard, is paddled ashore, remaining attached to the dory by a length of buoyant line which has a telephone cable core. On the return run the procedure is reversed, dinghy back to dory and dory to MTB. The key to the last of these stages is the use of a radio 'S' phone operated by one of the signallers. The latter, with the set strapped to his chest, has to stand up and tune in to a steady stream of 'talk' broadcast from the parent ship. As the signaller turns around, his body acts for a small part as a screen which blanks out reception. The centre point of this blank is the direction in which to 'home'. Such, briefly, is the theory.

Apart from some nocturnal practising off and on an Ostende beach, we had little to do apart from getting to know each other – also a useful exercise. There was much hospitality aboard the MTB, and from some undiagnosed source a jeep materialised thus allowing a visit or two to Bruges, some 15 miles away. Sometimes it was almost possible to forget that more serious business lay ahead.

The first recce was scheduled for Friday 13 and we made all due preparations with up-to-the-minute care. However the weather turned sour and there was a postponement for two nights. We had been given a long and detailed questionnaire about the Walcheren gap and its surroundings to which – with rather more than a touch of optimism – someone was expecting answers. We were warned again about the ferocious tides to be expected, so that it became increasingly obvious, the more we thought about it, that the dory, capable of a mere five-and-a-half knots, might quite probably be swept helplessly through the gap into the centre of Walcheren. Also, with a nice touch of psychological ineptitude, we were told the actual date of the assault – 1 November – at the same time being given strict orders that we were on no account to be taken prisoner, to which was appended the information that one of our agents on Walcheren had just been caught and interrogated under torture. As we had no cyanide pills to hand, we were not unduly sorry to know of Hitler's special order that all Commando soldiers captured on raids were to be summarily shot and not treated as prisoners of war. All of which meant, so far as I was concerned, that my normal quota of pessimism took a marked downward tumble.

It was a calm, moonless night as we cast off in Ostende, the powerful throb of the engines quickening rhythmically as we passed the harbour mouth and met the open sea. Duly, off Walcheren, the MTB stopped, 1,200 yards offshore. Even in the dark we could make out the dunes, the tower at Westkapelle, the gap itself. Noiselessly the dory was dropped and we started to clamber aboard. Then suddenly a light began flashing from the tower – a series of AAA, no doubt an attempt to call us up. We were promptly recalled by Keep and the dory was raised clear of the water, allowing the MTB to move away quietly at half-speed. Then four searchlights opened up, one illuminating the gap itself. We were soon caught in one of the beams, but Whitby at once made smoke and only one shell and a few rounds of tracer were loosed off at us. The searchlights continued their probing until we were seven miles out to sea and on our way back to Ostende.

On the night of the second recce the weather was churlish from the start. In fact, we learned later that the forecast had been so bad that Coastal Forces had cancelled operations. As the MTB headed up the coast from Ostende, the nasty swell and rising wind were decidedly ominous, and when we slowed to position six cables offshore, it was obviously blowing up for a thoroughly dirty night. The engines stopped, the red light came on and conversation tailed off to whispers. Over his charts the navigating officer gave me bearings for getting back to Ostende in the event of our having to fend for ourselves in the dory.

'Just in case,' he laughed apologetically. 'It's just possible they might come in handy.'

'Thanks a million,' I replied. 'Try and keep some bacon and egg for us for breakfast.'

The dory engine throbbed into life and we cast off from the MTB. Moments later we were in complete darkness. Now we had only the compass to guide us to the gap – somewhere in the blackness ahead. We were not to know until afterwards that shortly after we had left, because of the worsening weather, Keep, on the MTB, had tried to recall us on the walkie-talkie – and failed.

It was so black that we could make out no silhouettes ashore, and from the first we really stood little chance of finding the gap. We got in among fairly heavy surf and may indeed have been in the gap itself, but we could not be sure. We ran down the coast on a compass bearing for some minutes, with no result, then turned back and found ourselves in surf once again. We decided therefore to land and five of us paddled off in the rubber dinghy. We soon realised, however, that we were coming no closer in to the shore and to our dismay, after not many minutes, we were told on the buoyant line telephone that almost 500 yards of the cable had been run out. Our paddling had been in vain: the fierce tide must have been sweeping us along parallel to the shore. Landing would have been impossible. We were not surprised, when we got back to the dory, to be told that its own kedge warp had been 'strumming like piano wire'. It was as well that it was made of good strong stuff.

A long run up the coast eastward in the dory, against the tide, proved fruitless and another, equally pessimistic, return run no better. By this time it was raining and blowing really hard, turning into the thoroughly disagreeable night we had anticipated. At 1.30am we decided to admit defeat and return to the MTB. And that – perhaps not surprisingly – was easier said than done. On the first run out to sea there was no response on our signaller's homing set, nor could he get through on the walkie-talkie. Attempt after attempt proved futile. Then the Germans started jamming and made further efforts useless. After some 20 minutes we began to circle and even tried another run in shorewards, but still with no success. By now the sea was so rough that we were beginning to ship water, green, cold and uncomfortable. At 2.15am we decided that there was nothing for it and that we must attempt the 35 miles back to Ostende on our own. Those compass bearings given me by the navigating officer were not to be so superfluous after all.

And it was precisely at that moment that the engine petered out.

Its dying cough was pathetic, somehow matching my order 'Out paddles!' which no doubt in normal circumstances would have been greeted with hoots of derision: the prospect of paddling 35 miles through a welter of sea in our semi-waterlogged dory and just off a largely enemy-held coastline was singularly lacking in attractiveness.

Almost matter-of-factly the situation was saved. By the light of a pocket pencil torch – and one man's skill. Cpl Ron John knew everything there was to know about dories and their tantrums. He was the mechanical genius with our unit in Cornwall; now he came into his own. But how he brought the spark of life to that engine, its base slopping in inches of bilge water, in the dark and the rain and the cold, with everything at stake, I shall certainly never know. And how, in any case, did it just happen that he was carrying a pocket pencil torch? I can only reach for answers – with a profound sense of awe. Never again will I treat an ordinary pencil torch with contempt.

Dory-dinghy pairing as used in small-scale reconnaissance raids on enemy-held territory.

With an indignant grunt the engine restarted. In a few moments we were under way once again. Perhaps it was imagination, perhaps not, but the wind seemed to have dropped just a very little, the sea to be a fraction less hostile. Even so, with eight men and so much gear aboard, the dory had only a few inches of freeboard, and every wave seemed to add its quota to the increasing amount of water we shipped. I well remember how maddeningly difficult it was to do any baling, sitting hunched in six inches of sea water that kept slopping and slapping about my ankles, and underneath a spare jerrycan full of petrol, a telephone, a walkie talkie and half the engine cover. But if there were no particularly noticeable signs of comfort, at least the engine was beginning to sound out, however faintly, a distinct song of hope.

We surged and swayed drunkenly seawards and, once feeling confident that we were well clear of the coast, settled for 280 degrees, the first leg of the homeward course we had been given.

At 4.30am we reckoned it was time to change to the second leg, a bearing of 190 degrees, which theoretically should take us in to Ostende. It was more than two hours since we had made the decision to head for home. But this turned out to be much too optimistic, probably in part at least because the tide was still continuing to play nasty tricks on us. It very nearly landed us in deep trouble.

EYE TO THE HILLS

We found ourselves nearing the coast all right, but not approaching the surf and shingle beach we would have imagined and liked to find somewhere near Ostende. Surprisingly we made out land to starboard, not dead ahead, and we half-saw too the dim glow of a ship's light. At first we were completely nonplussed, then suddenly it dawned on us – we were inside the long arm of the mole at Zeebrugge. And Zeebrugge was at that time still in enemy hands. Fortunately, of course, it was still pitch dark and we managed to sneak well out to sea again without any unwelcome trouble.

At last the darkness lightened perceptibly and the sky began to grey up with the glimmerings of dawn. More and more clearly we were able to make out the monotonous line of the coast for the last slow miles – and maddeningly slow they seemed to be too, with the whole setting cheerless as only the North Sea can look on a bleak November morning.

And then it was all unforgettably different. At 9.30am we swung into the harbour at Ostende and slowed to a stop alongside the MTB. And there was everyone on deck, giving us an incredible, vociferous welcome. Yet not incredible really. The previous evening Whitby had told us as we moved off from the MTB into the Westkapelle darkness that to hang about waiting for us any later than 3.30am would be much too risky. In fact they had waited until 6.15. It had not been a happy run for them back to Ostende.

Three nights later we returned to the gap. Once again we were given strict orders not to be captured. This time it was a calm, still night and we were almost startled by the bark of the dory engine as it was brought to life at the dropping point. As we ran in, haze seemed to shut us in at once, while dory and dinghy were ringed by so much phosphorescence that it seemed certain we would be hopelessly conspicuous from any distance. We made our landfall some 400 yards east of the gap, turning to starboard towards it. We ran past it, making out the tower at Westkapelle, then turned back close to one of the groynes which run out to sea for 80 yards or so. Opposite the gap and perhaps 100 yards offshore we dropped the kedge and prepared to embark in the dinghy. Then suddenly we saw a light ashore, possibly from a pillbox slit, so we raised the kedge again and moved some 200 yards out to sea. We still hoped for a chance to land unnoticed, but the enemy were obviously very jumpy. They put up a series of verey lights, making everything so bright we failed to understand how they could miss seeing us. We made our way back therefore to the MTB – no homing failure this time, only the same eerie comet-tail of phosphorescence astern of the dory, which again we felt sure could only be startlingly obvious to the Westkapelle batteries. But nothing untoward happened. We muscled up the scrambling net on to the welcoming deck of the MTB, with the dory close on our heels hoisted inboard on the davits. Whitby waited quietly for several minutes to make a few observations of the tide, and it was only when the engines grumbled into life and we began to move off that the four searchlights opened up. Trained on the shoreline, they seemed to be making sure that the gap had dazzling prominence centre stage.

At the time we paid little heed to the irony. We were much more interested in the luxury of the MTB ward-room. The run back to Ostende was uneventful.

Although we had never set foot on Walcheren, the Brigadier seemed pleased enough with such information as we had obtained: scrappy details regarding the searchlights and batteries, outline of the gap, vagaries of the tides and so on. I doubt all the same if the long questionnaire which we had been given in the first place could ever have been answered at all satisfactorily.

On Walcheren D-Day, 1 November, I was able to watch the Westkapelle landings from the MTB, which was acting as 'messenger' for the headquarters ship, HMS *Kingsmill*. According to the original battle plan, the landings were to have been preceded by an intensive bombing raid by the RAF. Most unfortunately the weather was too uncertain and the raid had had to be called off. A preliminary bombardment was in fact carried out by HMS *Warspite* and the ageing monitor *Erebus*, lying offshore, but the LCT (T)s used in the assault were still desperately vulnerable, easy slow-moving targets for the shore batteries, and the cost in lives was tragically high.

Meanwhile some of our St Ives party had been detailed to help in the assault on Flushing, mainly to cope with any sea-wall climbing involved, and had moved the previous night from Ostende to Breskens. Captured by a Canadian brigade several days previously after particularly tough fighting, Breskens had become a useful 'pocket' on the Scheldt as the key take-off point for the crossing to Flushing.

Tragically the small party fared badly. On the run in, the bow ramp of the assault landing craft jammed open, thus removing its protective cover, Cpl John, though wounded in the knee (and later decorated with the Military Medal), managed to get it closed, but not before Lieut. Syd Richardson was killed by a burst of enemy fire.

Syd had been an immensely keen member of the St Ives team, particularly happy to have taken part in two of the recces. So it was that later that November it was my task to visit his parents in Lancashire. Syd was just 21 and an only son. It was the most difficult mission I have ever had to undertake.

Was it nearly 60 years ago – or was it yesterday?

Chapter Eleven

MIXED BAG

ONE way and another the years that followed the war had in them much that was grim and earnest. No settled job had been kept in cold storage, waiting to give me a welcome home. Cash flow was relentlessly downhill, while an ill-fitting demob suit with Al Capone hat to match, supplemented by a piggy-bank gratuity, did little to boost morale.

I now had two Helens, wife and daughter, to care for, and in 1952 son John came along as well; great days in one way, yet with worries hardly far to seek.

One spare-time avenue which did suggest itself, away from the one or two full-time jobs which had no obvious futures, was Saturday sports reporting. At least this would help in a small way to keep a rather hungry wolf from the door.

During the war I had taken part in a football 'friendly' against a police team on the vast acreage of Hampden. Recollections of this pinnacle of achievement and of my debut as a newshound long before, when I had reported a mannequin parade in Norwich, filled me with unwonted confidence and sent me to the sports desk of the Glasgow *Evening Citizen*. Surprisingly success came at once. I was set to covering 'Alliance' league matches – 50 words on the first half of the game plus the names of the second half scorers and the final result. Payment a princely five shillings.

In due course this took me to some far-flung grounds and such non-vandalised phone boxes as could be discovered. Occasionally better things did come my way. One Saturday I was sent to cover a charity match, once again at Hampden. I duly made my way to the luxurious press box, a rather more comfortable location than the touchline stances to which I had been growing accustomed. Spotting a vacant seat at the spacious window overlooking the pitch far below, I quickly made for this vantage-point.

'Hey, you'd better not sit there,' muttered a fellow scribe, a note of awe in his voice. 'That's Waverley's seat.' The warning was just in time. The door swung open and in stalked the great man himself, cigar brandished majestically aloft, astrakhan collar turned up against the cold. His reports, I concluded, must have brought in more than five shillings a time.

Fortunately things took a turn for the better when I became rugby correspondent. There were, of course, still matches to report with none of the Hampden luxury. Standing on a touchline at Fort Matilda to watch Greenock Wanderers in driving sleet was an afternoon ploy with remarkably little to commend it. But great was the compensation –

reporting on internationals at Twickenham and Lansdowne Road (sadly never at Cardiff Arms Park or in Paris), and on several occasions at Murrayfield. What matter if at that particular time Scotland was mostly lacking in Grand Slam potential?

One Glasgow Saturday stands clear in memory. My afternoon's assignment was to cover two club matches, one at Old Anniesland, the other just round the corner at New Anniesland – the main entrances a fair distance apart and with no short cut known to me, if indeed any existed. There was, however, an intervening iron fence, tall and topped with long, sharp spikes clearly just made for scaling; no more than a trifling inconvenience to a veteran of war still sound in wind and limb.

All went well till I stood atop the railing. Confidently I jumped. And one leg remained behind. It had been caught with a spike through a trouser turn-up. How long I hung ignominiously impaled head downwards I cannot recall. All I know is, I struggled free at last, and my mission was accomplished at both matches.

Fortunately as time went on sports reporting lost much of its significance. My hopes came to focus much more keenly on writing about the outdoors. Opportunities for this did come along, but painfully slowly; markets – in Scotland at least – were scarce in those first post-war years. Today's explosive exodus to hill and loch and coast was only just beginning to be imagined.

The best, most important breakthrough came in 1946, when my first *Scottish Field* article appeared. It was the start of an association that was to last for the next 40 years. Over that hugely varied, enjoyable timespan I was to work for six successive editors, privileged after a while to write my own column on subjects of personal choice, also at times writing under the names of John Murray and Donald Mackintosh, since one editor was unwilling to include more than one piece by the same person. There were, of course, an increasing number of opportunities to contribute elsewhere, while I was busy on books as well. In short, life gradually took on a much brighter hue.

Then, too, housed as we were in Glasgow, we even managed after a while to acquire a car, so bringing the hills that little bit closer.

Family holidays usually took us to Speyside and a particularly happy base at Dulnain Bridge, thus providing plenty of chances to get still better acquainted with the Cairngorms and Monadh Liath. Work too allowed a fair amount of travelling. Sometimes in October there would be an oddly convenient excuse to visit Aberdeen – over the old Devil's Elbow and aside to the tops overlooking Loch Callater, dinner in Braemar, then maybe a bivouac among the Deeside pines, or on down the road by the river, savouring the birches in their autumn splendour under a full moon.

Unexciting Munro-bagging maybe, yet giving of much enjoyment. Mayar, for instance, at the head of Glen Isla, romped over one July evening, leaving Glasgow at 5pm and home to bed by 2am. Or another summer evening from the Devil's Elbow – eight tops, four of which Munros – the *pièce de résistance* of the walk hearing a huge herd of deer 'talking' away together before I came over a ridge of the moor and surprised them in their bedded-down hundreds.

During the war much of our cliff-climbing had deliberately been done by night, always with the proviso that there had to be a half moon or better. Sometimes, of course, it would be unpleasant enough, with mist perhaps and the foghorn at Pendeen sounding out its dreary monotone. But sometimes, too, with the moon at the full, over Land's End maybe, the whole Atlantic out beyond the Longships would be rippled silver reaching away to infinity.

And so it seemed the thing to do to try some night outings as a peacetime ploy. The harvest moon was exactly right for the Buachaille's Curved Ridge with Norman Easton. An enormous orange climbed up somewhere behind the Bridge of Orchy and Blackmount hills, floodlighting our stairway. We mounted quickly to the Crowberry Tower and Buachaille's cairn, then turned and rattled down the ridge again to the Coupall and a midnight bathe, before dossing down to as comfortable a couch as I've known in deep, dry heather.

A March moon was different – in every way except for enjoyment. Norman Tennent, Bill Clarkson and I sat it out till midnight over coffee and sandwiches in the lounge of Lochawe Hotel. The night porter was puzzled, no way impressed by our appearance; relief at our departure was not heavily disguised.

Up in the snow-bowl of Cruachan's eastern corrie it was like day. The sky was cloudless, the moon shining brilliantly free. The silence would have been eerie had it not all been so pleasant, and as we each made our separate ways up the ideally crisp snow to the ridge, not even the occasional grunt was disturbing.

There was no suggestion of cold as we roamed westwards along the ridge, savouring to the full a whole unreal world of black and white. We visited five of Cruachan's seven tops, dropping down eventually from Stob Dearg, ravenous for the breakfast which friends living near Taynuilt had kindly agreed to treat us to.

Another night – this time of brief darkness during a heatwave weekend in late May. Theo Nicholson and I had crossed to Rum on the *Lochmor* from Mallaig and pitched our tent on a grassy strip by the shore of Loch Scresort. We had previously obtained permission to land from Lady Bullough, who at that time owned the island, and had duly been given a genial welcome by the head keeper.

Shortly before midday we left camp to do the classic traverse of the magnificent Rum ridge – an expedition which, according to the *Guide Book*, should take approximately eight hours, thus bringing us home comfortably for supper.

We arrived back for breakfast the following morning, having been away for 20 hours.

What I remember most clearly about the walk is the oven heat. Theo was carrying a water-bottle filled with neat orange squash and every time we came across a trickle of water this was diluted and we had another drink. By the day's end – after the splendid tops of

Fine country for Munroists. The hills of Knoydart beyond Loch Quoich.

Allival and Askival, Trallval, Ainshval and Sgurr nan Gillean – the last sensation of orange had gone. Making a rather foolish choice at the far end of the ridge, instead of dropping down eastwards to the Dibidil path, we decided to go north-west and ended down at Harris, on the 'wrong' side of the island. The result was kinder than we deserved; a cup of tea and sandwiches from a young shepherd and his wife, several hours' sleep in the deep hay of their barn, then a half-awake trudge of six miles back to camp and breakfast.

Further island-going round about that time getting material for my pen – a not uncongenial kind of work – took me to a whole scattering of West Coast islands from Ailsa Craig to Handa and St Kilda, almost all new to me.

For a first visit to Mull I had what I thought was the brilliant idea of bivouacking at the summit cairn of Ben More. The weather, however, would have none of it and blanketing mist made quite sure I would enjoy no entrancing island panorama, either at sunset or at dawn. I enjoyed the evening ridge-wander all the same, over A'Chioch and up to the main top, contentedly dropping down again thereafter to bed down among the bog myrtle and the midges at lower level beside Loch na Keal.

Seen across the silver strip of Corryvreckan from the highest point of Scarba (first of the 'new' islands to be visited) the rumpled moors and distant Paps of Jura issued an irresistible invitation. It was a while, however, before it could be answered, with the plan of attack developing into a complicated 'stepping-stone' marathon. Given the only dates available, this simply had to work out right, as my extraordinarily trusting companion, Richard Baxter, had only just time to fit it all in before sitting an important exam.

Jura is nearly 30 rough miles in length, with the most obvious attractions, the Paps, lying well down towards the south-west corner. It would be scarcely feasible to work down the island, climb the Paps and return the same way. The only sensible finish seemed to be to traverse the hills and drop down to the ferry across to Port Askaig. By crossing Islay as well by the early bus next morning, it should, we decided, be quite possible to catch the homeward-bound steamer at Port Ellen.

It all began on Luing, on Johnnie Livingston the boatman's floor, where we had slept the night. Johnnie put us ashore among the seaweed beyond Jura's north end, after which we walked the morning away as far as Ardlussa, 10 miles on. Here the local laird spotted us and after very kindly entertaining us to long cool drinks on his front lawn, encouraged us further by taking us five more miles in his Land-Rover.

We still had a fair amount of walking to do before tackling the Paps, and even with the help of another brief lift it was 3pm before we left the road beside the Corran River. According to the *Guide Book* 'To climb all three peaks is a good day's work and involves at least 5,000 feet of ascent.' In fact we called it a day after Beinn Siantaidh (2,477ft) and Beinn an Oir (2,571ft), Jura's highest. Near the top of the latter, rain which had been threatening suddenly struck at us like spray from the bows of a speedboat, so that a second dip and re-ascent of a further 1,200 feet to the third of the Paps, Beinn a' Chaolais (2,407ft) had singularly little attraction. Instead we dropped to the moor and the final five rough miles to the ferry to Islay at Feolin.

Once again our virtue was rewarded when we knocked on a solitary cottage door. In borrowed plus fours and a kilt belonging to the absent head of the house in place of our sodden rags, we were set down to a memorable high tea, while our hostess phoned to summon the ferryman across from Port Askaig. Next day, after distinctly welcome bed and breakfast, we travelled homewards, south by bus to Port Ellen, while the plus fours and kilt returned by ferry again northwards, back to their rightful owner.

With the phenomenal upsurge of interest in outdoor activities after the war, the need for an efficient mountain rescue service grew steadily more urgent. Times had certainly changed since 1928 and the building of the memorial Ben Nevis hut, specially equipped with detachable shutters on which any occasional climbing casualties could be carried down to Fort William.

Apart from several search and rescue outings, my part overall was undistinguished. That is until 3am on a particularly cold winter's morning when the phone roused me from a deep and dreamless sleep. Living in Glasgow, I had been given the task of phoning the key person responsible for the district where an accident had occurred and asking for a whip round for volunteer rescuers to turn out and help. On this occasion there had been an accident on The Cobbler, so the nocturnal request was from the Arrochar police for me to arrange for the necessary help.

'Well, yes,' I replied, trying to fan a flicker of competence into life. 'Yes, indeed. But seeing this is Saturday, I imagine there must be plenty of climbers in Arrochar already, perfectly willing to help.'

'Excuse me, sir,' came back the voice, 'but this is Wednesday.'

There were, of course, more serious climbing days in that dim and distant past, if hardly as many as I would have liked. One that is certainly not dim in memory is Chancellor Gully in Glencoe, with Tom MacKinnon, Hamish Hamilton and George Roger – as strong a trio to trail along behind as anyone could have wished. The following is the account I wrote up afterwards for the Scottish Mountaineering Club *Journal* of April 1950.

*****

Our mood was frivolous – which probably explains why Hamish was allowed to have his way. He was all for exploring the long gully which scores the face of Am Bodach, eastern top of the Aonach Eagach. Easily distinguishable by the slanting, square-cut chimney which hangs above it at mid-height, this gully at first follows an obvious course, then a leftward trend higher up obscures its finish near the base of the Chancellor. It is well seen as one rounds the corner at the cottage beyond the Study, although even from here its great length cannot be properly appreciated.

It appeared that Hamish had been yearning for years to launch a serious assault and could not understand why nobody else had thought of it first. We could think of any number of likely reasons and were not slow to elaborate them. But it was all to no purpose, and in the end we resigned ourselves to an afternoon of futility.

By way of a gesture to the light-heartedness of our approach, we began by climbing through the culvert under the main road. As, however, the great drought of 1949 had been running its course for many weeks, this pitch was not more than moderate. Nor was the more orthodox entrance to the gully – a staircase up polished rock, wet with spray and brown as Munich beer – less than five minutes above the road. At least we could not complain of being tired out before we started.

Hamish and Tom had set off at a rollicking pace, but they soon discovered that even the outer defences of this formidable gully had to be treated respectfully. Their speed slackened, and at Pitch 2 George and I caught them up. Thereafter we worked closely together, finally linking up as a quartet.

Both of the first two pitches gave a spicy foretaste of what was to come, the second a steep tussle on unhelpful holds, with water splashing playfully past the left ear, then a 30-foot corner, smooth as the side of a bath, with one satisfying handhold for the final grasp and heave. With varying degrees of agility and grace we surmounted the obstacles in turn and emerged into the amphitheatre above. Then we came to a halt.

Pitch 3 looked as though it had nothing to commend it. The central waterfall – 90 feet of slimy bulge – was obviously out of the question, while it needed no second glance to size up the severities on the left. On the right – where Hamish put in his attack – there seemed little more comfort, with loose, wrongly sloping holds leading to a vertical vegetable garden. After some 40 feet of tenacious struggle there was plainly nothing for it but a rope from above, and Tom accordingly made his way aloft by a heather buttress on the right. Even with this help, which could not be given from directly above, the final manoeuvring looked highly sensational. It must be admitted that the pitch is not a pleasant one.

It was about this point that we began to grow seriously alarmed at the state of Tom's trousers. I have no doubt that, when originally found, these still showed traces of workmanlike construction, though when their prime was, probably not even their owner could have said. Earlier on in the day we had noticed certain rather ominous signs of things to come, but we had not been prepared for the wholesale disintegration which now began to set in. Hamish, in the lead, was spared the full significance of this tragedy, but for George and myself there was no averting of the horrified gaze. Facts must be strictly adhered to, even if the veil which we would so gladly have drawn must take its discreet place in the record of our subsequent doings.

Facing our troubles resolutely, George and I followed up the next two pitches. Number 4, with its awkwardly spaced holds, turned out to be a deceptive 24-footer right in midstream, whereas its successor, though longer, was comparatively easy by way of a right-hand alternative. They led to broken ground at the leftward bend in the gully – if we had but known it, a breather before the real business of the day.

So far the climbing had been rather reminiscent of Clachaig Gully, though not so deep-set into the mountainside. Now its character changed. Instead of continuing narrow and shut in, the gully half opened, letting its left wall sweep skywards in a huge curtain of slabs. Momentarily I thought of Idwal, without the scars and scrapes of the great Welsh trade routes. Here was something worth waiting for, something to provide that *pièce de résistance*, or else bolt, bar and seal the door on the whole climb.

Forty feet up there was a sill, and Hamish, the light of battle in his eye, lost no time in working up to it. Then, as soon as he had been joined by Tom, he set off leftwards towards a brown-lichened boss and the steeper face above. As George and I waited and watched, we could see that there was a dour enough battle going on, and 100 feet of rope were run out before Hamish, moving with the stealth of a cat burglar, crept over the crowning gutter.

Tom chose to follow the watercourse route to the right. No doubt he had some reason for this, best known to himself, but he evidently had cause to regret it. A succession of grunts and unintelligible monosyllables marked the stages of his upward progress, which appeared to consist of balance moves on a vertical ladder of ferns. It was with some relief that we watched him complete this variation with a heave that landed him like a spent salmon beside Hamish. There was no need to wait until he had recovered his breath to

Chancellor Gully, the long rock-climb scarring the face of Am Bodach, Glencoe.

realise that his recommendation would have been for the 'fresh air' route; George and I would have chosen it in any case.

I am reliably informed that the pitch that followed the Great Slab was one of the hardest of the climb, but truth compels me to admit that I remember nothing of it. I have a clearer picture of the pitch above, an awkward rib which took us to yet another lofty slab. On the latter we became reprehensibly strung out at the full extent of our two ropes without any obvious safeguard. The 'thinnest' section occurred at three-quarter height, and it was with pardonable anxiety that we watched the vanguard work up it, then cross to better holds on the right. The idea of defeat here, with little help for roping down, was singularly unattractive, and the eye travelled with ominous ease down the grey sea of slabs at our feet. As if to stir the imagination still more, one or two fragments of rock spun past us with an angry hum.

Up to this point the outcome of the climb had been in doubt. Had the final moves on this second big slab been more exacting than the middle section, we might have had to retreat. Not that withdrawal would necessarily have involved descent of the whole gully, for, unlike some other routes of comparable length and difficulty, escape seemed quite feasible at a number of points. But it would have been failure which, after coming so far, would have been particularly bitter.

Once above the slabs, however, we knew for certain that all would be well. The gully narrowed to form a dank grotto with a great grey central fin, wet and slippery, but now without exposure. There was obviously nothing here to stop us and, as he straddled merrily up the knife edge, Hamish seemed almost to be purring for sheer delight.

Still this amazing gully led up and on, but easily now and ending at last with a huge chock-stone blocking the way. Fortunately this had a mossy covering that was agreeably stable and we stepped from it to an ample platform of turf and scree. As we coiled the ropes and relaxed in a comfortable glow of satisfaction, we thought back on the details of the afternoon – in particular that, almost by accident we had chosen the gully at all and that we had discovered not just that it would go, but go with supreme enjoyment from start to finish.

We made our way leisurely up screes to the ridge east of the Chancellor and duly reached the cairn of Am Bodach. It was a dull, mild evening and all colour was drained from the views. Nevis and the Mamores had a parched, barren look about them, and westwards the island hills had the unreality of shadows. It was too late to rest long and soon we were far down the eastern corrie on the way to the road. The day's last memory is of dinner at Inverarnan, a battle between sleepiness and the greed inspired by an enormous dish of blaeberries and cream.

*****

In the story of Scotland's hills an altogether unique place may be said to belong to the hotel at Inverarnan and the Girvan family, its owners for just over 40 years, from 1930 until 1971.

Inverarnan Hotel at the foot of Glen Falloch, once beloved of outdoor enthusiasts, not least for Girvan family hospitality.

After the interminable bends on the old Loch Lomond road, to Tarbet and on beyond Ardlui, the hotel was an ideal stopping-place on the way north up Glen Falloch to the hills. Perhaps, all the same, it could have best been described as a place of contrasts – heart-warming welcomes and not seldom frozen pipes; log fires and bed-springs that twanged like clarsachs; unique informality and underlying very real competence. All of that we discovered to our delight in the early thirties. And wartime changed nothing. In the later years Inverarnan became even more the West of Scotland Mecca for a wide yet close-knit company of enthusiasts – climbers, hill-walkers and skiers.

Calling at Inverarnan, whether briefly in passing or for a longer stay, was always an event of special pleasure. In minutes after the welcomes from Nancy and Hannah there would be exchanges with them of news of all the 'regulars'. No matter how rushed the time of day, a pause for bazaar talk was never a nuisance for them. And if arrival happened to be after the start of the Friday evening meal, entrance into the dining-room would mean for the great or the good a pause in the buzz of talk and something akin to a sitting ovation. As immediate news was shared, more than just a ripple of interest would go round the room, after which the company would fall to once more upon the ample banquet before them, working heroically towards the favourite climax of pavlova and/or a ruthless attack on the big Stilton alluringly set on its own central table.

Mornings, while Nancy filled flasks and Hannah prepared a staggering mound of sandwiches, would be loud with talk of the day's programmes. Late afternoon was the time for high drama, with ferocious speeding down Glen Falloch, ice or no ice, to be back in time to bag one of the two baths likely to produce hot water. How death on the road was defied for so long no one ever knew.

In the evening – usually by invitation (and no way forgetting the lasses either) at the Girvans' own fireside in the 'den' – there would be a lively going over of the day's delights: in Glencoe, maybe, or on Beinn Laoigh, an ecstatic 'thousand feet of solid ice'. Or latecomers would come in off the hill long after dark, as often as not one of the party George Roger, beaming exuberantly and proclaiming to all and sundry how enjoyably 'the summit was attained'.

New Year was special. A *ceilidh par excellence*, with much dancing in the big lounge and the traditional oratory, George's annual 'engyne' declamation, Bob Grieve's unbeatable *Tam o' Shanter*. At midnight Nancy and Hannah would appear bearing genteel trays of sherries (although it has to be admitted, there would already have been reasonable discreet bedroom exchanges of malts). Then the usual wishing and kissing and *Auld Lang Syne* and further splendid oratory and song.

Sadly in 1966 the Girvans decided that winter closing had become necessary. The writing was on the wall. Five years later Nancy and Hannah shut the doors for the last time. Another ten years on Bill Murray was to write in Nancy's obituary, 'None of us will again know hospitality like hers… She and Hannah are associated still in our hearts and minds with the happiest days of our lives.' Many of us there are who would echo those words. A very special era, one of the most memorable chapters in the story of our hills, had come to an end.

*****

As a family, in the first dozen years after the war, we looked in on Inverarnan often enough. Whenever we could and no other attractions came in the way we escaped from the city to treat ourselves to another brief helping of Girvan hospitality. And never once were we disappointed. All in all, the future looked like continuing set fair.

Climbing Chancellor Gully, July 1949; George Roger, an Inverarnan enthusiast of the past.

Then suddenly, without warning, our sky darkened. In the autumn of 1957 my wife Helen was diagnosed as having ovarian cancer.

Elsewhere – in the last chapter of the book – I tell again something of the five long and heartbreaking years which followed: hospitals and operations, operations and hospitals, hopes raised, hopes dashed, faith relentlessly attacked. The end of the way an evening in September 1962.

Of the desolation and bleakness which followed and its bearing on a particular aspect of what was then the future I also tell later. Suffice it to say here that in our deep trouble we could not have received more thoughtfulness or more encouragement from other members of the family or from innumerable friends. Kindly looked after at home, we even received the gift of an Easter week in Austria, a break which seemed completely unreal, yet which played its part in that slow, sometimes imperceptible build-up of fresh hope for the future.

Oddly enough – or maybe most appropriately – it was Inverarnan which was the setting most intimately bound up with a very special turn of events four years later. Hogmanay there had been unusually enjoyable – the principal ingredient a young lady with a guitar and an irresistibly magic voice. Some time before – with intent, perhaps! – I had been introduced to Maisie (or more often Mais) and we had been meeting now and again, not unacceptably; once we had even escaped for half-an-hour together on our own.

Maisie too knew Inverarnan well, as on many occasions previously she had stayed there for climbing days and had come to know almost all the various 'regulars'. It was in no way surprising that she should have been in demand as a performer in that cheery log-fired lounge at Hogmanay.

Next day, walking near Loch Dochart, she nobly agreed to take me on. No less recklessly perhaps, I was venturing to take on a 'teuchter'; was not the Mackintosh motto 'Touch not the cat without a glove'? The following day we climbed Meall Corranaich – first of so many great hill-days together.

That year, 1966, was exceptional in another way also – we had two holidays abroad. Mais and I were married on 1 April – significant date – and after a brief visit to Vienna continued on our honeymoon travelling to Carinthia and a village named Bad Kleinkirchheim. There we felt in duty bound to attempt one of the local heights, so we chose the Strohsack, a peak of 6,247 feet. The weather was kind, the approach by a forest track of suitably gentle gradient. We are both convinced that we started on this adventure; whether or not we ever reached the summit neither of us has any idea.

Later that same year on a family holiday in the Roussillon district of southern France, we were able to climb Le Canigou (9,150 feet), a peak perhaps best described as an offshoot Pyrenee. This involved a night at a half way hut-hotel (readily forgotten on account of the miserably cramped sleeping quarters and one unpleasant stomach upset) and the compensation next day of a hot Munro-like hill traverse.

Yet, thinking back to 'real' Alpine days, it has to be confessed that since the war there have been plenty of occasions when, like the late C.E. Montague in his essay *Up to the Alps*, one could not help picturing the train as it climbed towards the heights and thinking wistfully 'And I not there, and I not there.'

Austria did in fact provide one reasonable exception, a thoroughly enjoyable couple of days during a brief visit to Neustift, in the Stubaital. This was a traverse of the Wilder Freiger (11,214ft), in good weather nothing of a problem, but still a worthy introduction to a fine corner of the Tyrol.

A bus to Ranalt and a long afternoon walk took Theo Nicholson, Maurice Cooke and me up to the Nürnberger Hut, where, warm, contented and drowsy after an ample meal, we spent the night. Dense mist blanketing our Alpine start next morning duly gave way to a brilliantly hot summer's day. The climb gave no trouble: high up, a long diagonal on snow-ice was running with water under the ravages of the sun; then rock and the final snowfield, tier upon sculptured tier to the summit, like the icing on a giant birthday cake.

In due course we dropped down to the box-like, unmanned Müller Hut on the Italian border. It was here, in September 1922, that Frank Smythe of early Everest days, along with two Austrians and a German, battered by a hurricane on the Wilder Pfaff, took refuge and had to spend three hungry nights before the storm eased. Our own further way, past the more luxurious Sulzenau Hut, was pleasantly easy, its finish at Ranalt just beating an evening thunderstorm.

After Austria – if one discounts Snowdonia as not exactly 'abroad' and some 'honest' climbing there to awaken memories – only Norway remains. From one of the Ben Nevis-sized hills on the fringe of the Jotunheim we looked over to the Beseggen Ridge, which Mais had traversed in that distant past before we met. This for her had followed the climbing of Norway's highest, Galdhöppigen (8,097ft), a summit attained, I am quite sure, with the express purpose of being able to make me envious in a then unknown, unforeseen future.

If climbs abroad were of no great significance, at least the home hills were providing much enjoyment. Most of the outings immediately after the war, through much of the fifties and again later on, were with Theo Nicholson. Theo had been a member of the 5th Scots Guards in 1940 and a fellow climbing instructor at Llanrwst in 1943, after which he went with the Lovat Scouts to Canada on ski-mountaineering training and later, still with the Lovats, to the fighting in Italy.

A real all-rounder, with a record – on foot and on ski – ranging over at least 10 countries, from Scotland, Norway and the Alps to the western United States and the South Island of New Zealand, Theo was always the best of companions on the hill, a close friend for exactly 50 years. Sadly, after ten frustrating months of ill health, he died in October 1992. The memories remain.

On the home hills doing what we enjoyed most – ranging far and wide over country new to us both rather than facing more gymnastic problems on rock and snow – made a long tally of days to remember. From Sutherland to Glen Affric, from the Fannichs to the

Ben Alder hills, the Easains, the Grey Corries and more besides, details tend to merge as the mists swirl and part.

One sunburning day from Invercauld took us over the many tops of Ben Avon and Beinn a' Bhuird, the two big eastern bulwarks of the Cairngorms, looked forward to ever since I had first devoured Seton Gordon's descriptions of them all of 30 years before. In the long day's wandering we met no one; only – at the cairn of Beinn a' Bhuird, I remember – a pair of dotterel showed us a typically fearless, friendly welcome.

The only really big disappointment was when we visited Knoydart in June 1954. We crossed from Mallaig with the mailboat to Inverie, in drenching rain, and spent two nights in the Torcuileainn bothy – according to my diary 'Two rooms, broken windows, leaky roof and concrete floors'. The day in between was one to match: 12 hours out and 7,500 feet of upward toil, all in mist as dense as it could be, over Meall Buidhe, Luinne Bheinn and Ladhar Bheinn.

In spite of which Knoydart still calls – sadly it has to be in vain.

Those magnificent hills hidden away in the hinterland between Kinlochewe and Dundonnell – once justly described as 'wilderness', now well trodden by Munroists – have given me of their best, in May 1958 and in July 1975.

The first foray, a satisfying wind-whipped marathon with Theo, took in that fine quartet with the names that read like random pickings from the Gaelic dictionary: A' Mhaighdean, Beinn Tarsuinn, Mullach Coire Mhic Fhearchair and Sgurr Ban.

It has to be confessed that it was partly on account of metrication that I paid my second visit to the area. This time, in a July heat-wave, was with my daughter Helen. Unlike her younger brother John, whose preference and prowess have regularly taken him to more level playing fields with a ball at his feet, Helen has always been in thrall to the hills. Inevitably – poor lass – in the early stages beneath the relentless parental eye, she had to put up with not a few wearisome slogs, but she got over that at a relatively tender age and came to relish fully all Scotland has to offer by way of rain, hail and shine. Joining the Ladies' Scottish Climbing Club gave her chances to visit the Alps and Arctic Norway with a number of kindred spirits. Then, in July and August 1970 she led a party of 12 fellow club members to Eastern Greenland, where they explored the peaks and glaciers of Natshorstsland, a little-known corner of mountainous territory opposite the more often visited Staunings Alps.

On the home hills Helen's Munro tally was nearing completion, but lacked some of the 'new' metricated summits. (My own attitude has always been that Sir Hugh's classic list should be sacrosanct and should be the recognised yardstick for Munroist qualification, right, wrong or doubtful). For us in the 'wilderness' there were two metric summits, Beinn a' Chlaideimh (3,000ft) and Ruadh Stac Mor (3,014ft), both new to me and, of course, satisfying for Helen.

After a late afternoon start from the east (a foolish choice) we had a tiring moorland approach to Achneigie bothy, then continued up Beinn a' Chlaideimh. We reached the top after sundown, to be rewarded with a magnificent western sky, mist-girdled, and a double brocken spectre. An hour and a half later, we were back down beside the river in Gleann na Muice, where, having no tent, we dossed down to our snouts in our sleeping-bags in a vain attempt to escape all the midges in Wester Ross. Next day, more sedately, we did the 'Big Red Stack', Ruadh Stac Mor, before a hot and seemingly endless bog-trot back to the car.

In due course, in September 1988, Helen's Munro celebration took place on Beinn Teallach, rather a featureless hill some three bleak miles north of the Loch Laggan dam which had scraped through to a place on the august list by 60.96 centimetres. The loyalty of Helen's supporters was impressive and a sizeable company gathered at the cairn. I suggested to her that as I had carried her up the last few yards of her first Munro when she was five, the least she might have done in return was to give me a lift on some of the steeper sections of the hill, but she was not a whit repentant.

My own ultimate Munro had fallen to a determined assault 12 years earlier, in April 1976. With its modest 3,062 feet, Fionn Bheinn near Achnasheen had seemed a sensible choice. Indeed, as the *Guide Book* put it: 'It must be one of the least inspiring 3,000ft tops in Munro's Tables, and can be climbed in just over an hour, without difficulty, from the road junction at Achnasheen'. Prudence had dictated that it should be kept to the last in case it might have necessitated Himalayan high camp tactics, including lusty porter support.

I had fondly imagined, of course, that so many of my friends would be eager to take part in this historic event that an admiring multitude would hasten to congregate at Achnasheen. In the event the assembly turned out to be rather less – in fact, only my wife and daughter. Some touches of interest were added to the walk by the birds we chanced to see – a few redwing seemingly in no hurry to return to Scandinavia, a cock ring ouzel, several golden plover and even a pair of eagles actually talking to each other as they circled. At the summit trig point, set at the edge of a cirque of Christmas cake cornices, the sun shone and the Arctic wind shrivelled, discouraging lengthy celebration. According to the historical record, the first successful addict, the Rev A.E. Robertson, was instructed to kiss the cairn of his final summit, then kiss his wife, who was with him. However, for my part I decided to play safe and gave Mais preferential treatment.

We are now eagerly looking forward to the third day of family celebration – when Mais herself reaches her first century. At the time of writing her total stands at 93 – near enough, even if for one of us at least the attainment of a paltry seven more suggests the advisability of a certain amount of haste.

Chapter Twelve

TWICE TOLD TALES 1 –
THE DINGHY AND
THE MOOR, 1958

AT a certain point in World War Two, while I was stationed in Cornwall, and some months before the Walcheren operation described elsewhere, it happened that I was detailed to give instruction in the use of the rubber dinghy.

Just how much concern this event caused the German High Command will probably never be known, but I think it would be fair to say that it occasioned me a good deal more. It was, after all, an army duty of some novelty, especially as those were days before the rubber dinghy had become commonplace. It was a duty for which I seemed particularly ill fitted, having never even seen a dinghy at close quarters until a couple of days previously.

However, I need not have worried. My success as a demonstrator was assured from the very first moment. Watched by my squad of earnest students, I stepped smartly into the dinghy off the sea wall of St Ives harbour and fell head first over the side into 14 feet of water.

Fortunately this did nothing to stifle in its infancy an affection for dinghying which after the war was to grow and flower as time went on. In Scotland especially there was clearly immense scope for adventuring just waiting to be enjoyed, and plans were certainly never wanting. There was only one snag and that not a small one – we had no dinghy.

Ready cash in those lean, far-off days was never exactly abundant, and the argument that a dinghy costing perhaps £50 or more topped the list of priorities in the family budget met with a singular lack of enthusiasm. Prowling round the shops had proved as useless as it was time-consuming. It had led eventually to a ship-chandler of some repute.

'Yes indeed, sir,' I was told, 'we have two or three different types of dinghy on offer. Where was it exactly you said your yacht was moored?' Progress had undoubtedly ground to a halt.

Then someone suggested putting the query to the editor of one of the yachting magazines, and the latter, most helpfully, directed me to Birkenhead, to a firm of air-sea equipment manufacturers. A few days later I had details before me of a new dinghy just about to be marketed: the 3Y Multi-purpose Inflatable Boat. This looked in the illustration exactly what I had been used to during the war and just what we were looking for now.

Prelude to adventure. The dinghy arrives and is unpacked.

Obviously it was the ideal end to the hunt. Only the persistent problem of finance remained.

Having got so far, however, a falter now was unthinkable. There was only one thing to do. I wrote another letter to Birkenhead, suggesting this time that, as I was unable to afford a dinghy, but had some interesting expeditions in mind, it might be possible to give me one. The reply was not the curt refusal I expected – and deserved; on the contrary, it exceeded all my hopes. I might, if I liked, have the 3Y on loan for one month. A sporting spirit must surely have prevailed round that Birkenhead boardroom table.

The great moment came at last when the dinghy was deposited with full pomp and ceremony at our door – a massive parcel of thick wrappings, endless string and protruding paddle-shafts. At once the younger members of the family fell upon it and literally tore the parcel to pieces. Quickly the contents were spread out in disarray on the garden lawn – black hull, plywood thwarts and paddles, bellows inflator, even a tin of repair solution. On first acquaintance the 3Y certainly looked a solid, serviceable job.

Sundry short experiments followed and one major expedition – a very damp trip down the River Endrick, which rises in the Fintry Hills in Stirlingshire and ends up in Loch Lomond. There still remained, however, some valuable days before the dinghy had to go back to Birkenhead, and one project seemed to me to be outstanding among the many – a crossing of the Moor of Rannoch.

EYE TO THE HILLS

On first consideration the merits of this idea are not perhaps particularly obvious; one thinks, after all, of Rannoch Moor as not much more than a vast expanse of heather, or as Dr John Macculloch graphically put it almost two centuries ago, 'an inconceivable solitude, a dreary and joyless land of bogs, a land of desolation and grey darkness'. But a look at the map quickly shows the error of this belief. A magnificent waterway is seen to stretch right across the Moor from the Glencoe road, via Loch Ba, the Abhainn (River) Ba and Loch Laidon, all the way to Rannoch railway station on the old West Highland line. Even the most unimaginative would surely admit that this looks a dinghy route of the highest order and one thoroughly well worth following.

As dinghy partner for this venture, I asked my cousin-in-law Lindley Carstairs if he would care for the job and was delighted when he agreed. He had been my companion on innumerable mountain days from Ben Hope in Sutherland to The Merrick in Galloway and from Kintail to the Braes of Angus. This, of course, would be an expedition of a different kind altogether, and Lindley's action in volunteering for the unknown seemed to me to be especially commendable.

We discovered soon enough that we had plenty of details to consider, for the plan of campaign was of necessity rather complicated. No road runs across the moor, only the railway line across its eastern edge, so that our return to base from our destination at Rannoch station would have to be by rail, with the dinghy duly deflated and stowed for carrying. The idea was therefore that we should leave Glasgow after work on Friday evening and drive in two cars to Bridge of Orchy station, which lies on the southern fringe of the moor some 15 miles south of Rannoch. There one of the cars would be left. We would then carry on together in the second car to the launching-point beside Loch Ba, which comes conveniently to within a hundred yards or so of the road. By that time it would be dark, but with some generous help from the moon we reckoned there should be little difficulty in travelling through the night. The point of doing the trip in this rather odd way was that there would be plenty of time to catch the Saturday morning train back from Rannoch to Bridge of Orchy, yet if things did go far wrong and we missed it, there would still be a comfortable margin before the afternoon train was due. There are no trains at all on Sunday and we had no wish to be stranded at Rannoch until Monday.

We eventually fixed on Friday of the autumn holiday, the last weekend in September, when there would be a full moon. Our decision was the signal for the usual breakdown in the weather. Each day of the preceding week seemed worse than the one before. Rain whipped the city streets and on some of the higher hills there was a peppering of the first snow-showers of the winter. On Wednesday the wind rose to a paroxysm of fury, while on Thursday even the weather forecast seemed as though it might be accurate for once: 'High winds with gales in places and frequent heavy showers; thunder at times.'

Then, on Friday, a sudden miraculous change set in. The wind dropped and the clouds dispersed. All day long the sun shone and in its warmth our faded optimism re-emerged and flourished anew. By the time Lindley and I were making our separate ways northwards in the evening the serenity of the sky gave a promise that looked unbreakable.

We met as arranged at Bridge of Orchy and in the gathering gloaming loaded all the gear into one car. As we moved off again, across the darkening moors and round the great curve and climb beyond Loch Tulla into sight of Loch Ba itself, we felt with a surge of elation that we were really under way at last.

There seemed to be something rather furtive about drawing off the road and starting to pump air into the unwieldy carcase of the dinghy. Lindley had brought a large electric carriage lamp, and into and out of its beam we moved like a couple of poachers at work on a clandestine gralloch. Frequently we found ourselves caught in the headlight glare of passing cars and we felt guiltily conspicuous as we crouched and fumbled at our task. The pumping seemed endless and during my spells of toil I found myself counting the strokes by hundreds, after the time-honoured manner of a step-kicker on a monotonous mountain snow-slope. In addition the two inlet valves gave a certain amount of trouble and in the end we had to leave off pumping with the pressure rather less than we should have liked. We sealed the valves doubly tight with balloon rubber and corks, then, hoping for the best, hoisted the dinghy in triumph shoulder high and moved off on our 100-yard carry down to the edge of the loch.

The night was very quiet and almost windless. Above the hunched shoulder of Beinn Creachan the moon was just up. Momentarily it was withdrawn behind a veil of cloud, but this was fortunately not so dense as to cause any anxious qualms. Already the lanes of silver which its light projected across the moor made striking contrast with the black corners of the loch. Against the peat at our feet the water lay absolutely still, as dark and mysterious as the contents of Gaelic coffee. Gingerly we lowered the dinghy to the bank and let it slip into the water.

I think it must have been just about this time that I first happened to notice my companion's hat. Up until then I had been concentrating on all the various preparations for the launching, but suddenly, in a moment of awful revelation, I became aware of what surmounted Lindley's head. In shape one might have said that it resembled an inverted casserole, or possibly that type of shako worn by some regiments of foot during the Peninsular War. Even in the moonlight I could see that it was made of some kind of hairy material, akin perhaps to coconut matting.

'What on earth is that?' I gasped.

'What's what?' replied Lindley, no doubt sensing the trace of anxiety in my voice.

'The thing on your head. Is it a spare bailing can or something?'

Lindley straightened himself up from contemplating the dinghy. 'I've been waiting for months for a suitable occasion to put on this hat and I think this is it. I'd have imagined you'd be the first to agree.'

'All right,' I said, as soothingly as I could. 'Wear the thing if you must, only I'd rather you occupied the rear seat in the dinghy if you don't mind.'

We pushed off, hat and all, at 8.20pm. As we paddled gently, almost hesitantly, away out of the inky black shadow of our inlet, there was a feeling of utter unreality about the whole venture. It was like the start of an operational sortie in wartime and one felt like talking in whispers, when in fact a shout would have gone unheard. The occasional squeaking of paddle-shafts meeting rubber seemed queerly out of keeping with the silence of the night.

The problem of Loch Ba, the first stage of our journey, was its extraordinarily complex maze of islands. They confronted us at once, some large, others mere boulder-reefs and shoals, round all of which it was hopelessly difficult to choose the right way to steer. The moonlight added to the deception, laying subtle traps in silver and black, while our eyes were still unused to measuring distances or gauging horizons. Several times we had to paddle back and choose a new avenue and once or twice we quite simply ran aground. Gradually, however, we made distance; now we could distinguish the familiar outline of Buachaille Etive Mor, blacker than the black sky, away over to the north-west; slowly but surely the car headlights on the road, ranging over the heather like lighthouse beams, fell farther and farther astern.

After half an hour or so we paused for a short rest and a bite of chocolate and fruit. We had steered well out toward the middle of the loch and laid down our dripping paddles without regret. Round us the water had the look of black ice, hiding unfathomable depths. We scarcely spoke, listening for preference to the silence. Utter quiet lay about us, save once only when we heard the sounds of a train in the distance, somewhere over the moor near the old Wood of Crannach. Such silence, I reflected, was infinitely worth a quest like this. What greater contrast could we have found to the daily round, to the time-menaced scurry of the city, than this brief rest on an Argyllshire lochan, motionless under the stars?

Our troubles with the islands were not yet at an end and soon after our restart we found ourselves involved once more. An avenue of silver, bright in the moonlight, looked as though it should be the way ahead, only to mock us like a will o' the wisp at the last moment by turning out to be an isthmus of sand. We made a sharp hairpin bend back to port only to find big boulders guarding another jutting point. Inevitably we cut the corner too fine and there was a harsh grating noise as the belly of the dinghy caterpillared over rough rock.

'Just as well it's made in two compartments,' I remarked, as we pushed off again and steered out into a deeper channel. 'If one half gets punctured the other is guaranteed to keep us afloat.'

'That's a comfort,' replied Lindley. 'I suppose I'd better take your word for it. Only, if I remember aright, that's what they said about the *Titanic*.'

Happily the argument was never put the test. We paddled on with optimism undimmed.

For some time now we had been looking ahead to the hill-slopes silhouetted against the eastern sky. Almost suddenly they seemed to be very much nearer. If, as now looked decidedly likely, they actually ran down to the moor between Loch Ba and Loch Laidon, then we must be very nearly at the end of the first stage of the journey. Our hopes certainly rose, and when the channel ahead narrowed to canal width, between banks fringed with moor grass, our paddle-strokes quickened expectantly.

Then unmistakably we heard the sound of a river. Here would be proof positive: if it was flowing out of the loch, it could only be the Abhainn Ba, the middle link in our chain. We nosed the dinghy against the bank and walked forward to prospect. Then, to avoid deception in the moonlight, we bent down and peered intently at the current. Yes, indeed, it was flowing east. Loch Ba was behind us and we were well ahead of schedule.

This was our point of no return. Once past here it would become progressively easier to carry on to Rannoch station, more difficult to work our way back to the Glencoe road. So we had decided in our planning beforehand. For, of course, we had always had to reckon with the possibility of unforeseen misfortune, such as hopelessly hostile weather or some mishap to the dinghy.

I put it to Lindley – knowing perfectly well what he would answer – that he might like to go back.

'No, indeed,' he said, looking round for a good place to hoist the dinghy from the water. 'That would be a poor idea. Let's see a bit more of Rannoch Moor.' I just hoped that what we did see of it during the next few hours would not be more than enough.

Between Loch Ba and Loch Laidon lies a stretch of moorland about a mile wide. Across this winds the connecting river, the Abhainn Ba, trending first south-eastwards, then slightly north of east. The difference in altitude between the two lochs is about 100 feet, so our hopes of being able to dinghy down were not at all high. What we saw merely confirmed our expectations. The Abhainn Ba was an honest Highland burn, some 15 yards wide, tumbling tunefully along through a maze of spray-flecked boulders. In the moonlight its channel looked thoroughly unwelcoming. There were no two ways about it: the moor ahead would need a long and exacting portage.

We re-stowed the gear in the damp depths of the dinghy and shoved in the paddles on top, then, taking an end each, we set off over the heather.

The sky had been scoured clear of the last shreds of cloud and the moon was riding free. Round us its light spilled in profusion over a sea of hummocks and hollows, the yellow autumn colours of the moor grass suggesting the sands of some limitless Sahara. At first the going was easy, over heather that was short, springy and obligingly level. Then it began to deteriorate. Ditch-sized burns kept crossing our path and every now and again the moonlight deceived us into stepping confidently on to the green moss of bogs. As we went squelching ankle-deep into the icy water, our gym shoes, damp before, became completely sodden and cold. Then the angles tilted and the ground became rougher. We met stiffer rises and, in between, deeper hollows, always set across our line of advance. Most of the latter contained peat-hags with steep or overhanging edges, and through them we slipped and slithered in erratic discomfort.

I could not help thinking once again of Dr John Macculloch's description, written apparently with some feeling more than a century and a half ago:

> Pray imagine the Moor of Rannoch; for who can describe it. A great level (I hope the word will pardon this abuse of it) 1000 feet above the sea, sixteen or twenty miles long, and nearly as much wide, bounded by mountains so distant as scarcely to form an apprehensible boundary; open, silent, solitary; an ocean of blackness and bogs, a world before chaos; not so good as chaos, since its elements are only rocks and bogs, with a few pools of water, bogs of the Styx and waters of Cocytus, with one great, long, sinuous, flat, dreary, black, Acheron-like lake, Loch Lydog, near which arose three fir trees, just enough to remind me of the vacuity of all the rest.

Under any circumstances crossing such country on foot is apt to be tiresome; when one is anchored inescapably to the end of a rubber dinghy, even less can be said in its favour. We tried changing hands and we tried changing ends; we tried hoisting the thing on to our shoulders, on to our backs, even on to our heads – all to no avail. There was no easy answer; we were shackled to our boat as inexorably as any pair of galley-slaves to their oar. And so there was nothing for it but to put up with it all, while muscles ached and throbbed and finally burned white hot in protest, with the torments of Burns's toothache:

> An' thro' my lug gies mony a twang,
>> Wi' gnawing vengeance,
> Tearing my nerves wi' bitter pang,
>> Like racking engines!

And then, quite suddenly, Loch Laidon was below us. Weary and out of breath, we topped a heather rise and there it lay, a narrow sheet of quicksilver reaching away into the dim background of the night. Thankfully we covered the last couple of hundred yards to its edge and shed our burden on a broad, grassy bank.

There we had our reward. We picnicked at the outflow of the Abhainn Ba, just below its last rollicking gallop over the boulders. The moon was at its brightest, high overhead, so that we could see every detail of the burn as it came racing downhill towards us in a torrent of tossing white foam. The night was still calm and pleasantly mild and so bright that we might almost have been sitting down to our morning elevenses, had the time been precisely 12 hours different. It was a relief after the encounter with the peat-hags to lean back and relax, and when Lindley produced a flask of coffee to go with our sandwiches, our comfort seemed complete.

After half an hour we bestirred ourselves once more. It would have been pleasant to stay and bivouac where we were, but we had agreed that it would be advisable to put as many as possible of Loch Laidon's five miles behind us during the night rather than wait until morning. Anything might happen to hold us up and we had no wish to finish the journey in a flurry of haste to catch the train. We therefore gathered together our gear, stowed it in a pile like the old clothes counter at a jumble sale, and launched away. Soon the song of the Abhainn Ba had begun to grow faint behind us.

Loch Laidon is comparatively narrow and deep in places, so we decided that it would be wise to keep within reasonable swimming distance of the shore. We chose the eastern side and soon were paddling along, close in, to a steady harmonious rhythm. The exercise kept us warm – except for our feet, which felt wet and cold beyond hope of recovery – and in addition we had the satisfaction of knowing that every hundred yards we 'stole' in this way represented another slice off the long stretch ahead of us in the morning.

That first hour of Loch Laidon was, for me at least, the most enjoyable of the whole expedition. For it alone, all our planning and all our toil would have been infinitely worthwhile.

There was still not a breath of wind to ruffle the mirror-surface of the water, and, with time mattering nothing, we slipped along almost without conscious effort. We rounded jutting promontories and passed bay after shingle bay backed by the silhouettes of heather banks. Scarcely a word was exchanged, for we were once again in a world of silence, silence so complete that we felt inclined to dip our paddles with stealth, as though to do otherwise would have been sacrilege. The moon was behind us and our own black shadows cut strange-shaped notches in the track of silver ahead. And above us blazed the stars in brilliant profusion, arching through the stupendous span of Plough and Pole Star to where Capella hung like an emperor's diamond near the scintillating crown of the Pleiades.

It was one of those nights which possess that quality of beauty so far beyond the power of words to describe. But our idyllic spell of paddling had to come to an end some time. Inevitably our arm muscles began to tire and as our strokes became more laborious, so gradually they lost rhythm – and pleasure. In addition a night breeze was at last springing up, blowing into our faces from across the bleak miles of the moor. Admittedly it was still gentle enough, but for all that it quickly furrowed the loch and despite all our protective clothing struck an icy chill. By 1.00am it had become obvious that it was high time for us to go ashore and bed down for what remained of the night.

It was not until we had shipped our paddles and stumbled unsteadily from the slopping puddle inside the dinghy that we realised how desperately cold we had become. Our legs almost creaked as we tried to straighten them, and our feet, now quite without feeling, seemed separated from us in a squelching, skidding world of their own. The landing-place we had chosen turned out to be much less sheltered than we had expected, for the ground immediately behind it was no better than a shallow scoop, floored with large angular boulders and scraggy heather that put one in mind of some corrie in the Cairngorms. In the midst of this paradise we tottered about, our teeth chattering, in the woolly hope that we might find a few level square feet on which to spread out our sleeping-bags.

Then, just at exactly the right moment, Lindley came to the rescue. From a hidden corner at the bottom of his rucksack he fetched out some Bovril and yet another flask, this time containing hot water. A few seconds later I had a steaming cup in my hand and could feel the comforting warmth literally flowing through me. That nightcap made all the difference just when it was most urgently needed.

The only drawback, I found, was that the glow did not extend to my feet. Even when I was able to thrust them far down into the depths of my sleeping-bag, they felt miserably like refrigerated lead. Nor was there much chance to improve matters at all by wriggling about; the ground underneath was so like a mountain scree-slope that the only way to stretch out was to insinuate oneself into a kind of narrow slalom course of boulders, in which a jerk one way bumped the right knee and a turn the other grazed the left elbow. I tried to console myself with Gino Watkins's dictum born on the Greenland ice-cap that 'mere cold is a friend, not an enemy', but the remedy had no marked success.

For compensation there was an outlook from our bivouac site of truly memorable beauty. We had fetched up directly opposite Eilean Iubhair, the 'yew tree island', and in the brilliant moonlight its outline lent variety to the silver of Loch Laidon and the dark contours of the moor. Loch Ba and the Abhainn Ba seemed very far away now, lost in obscurity beyond the bays and promontories we had just passed, but in silhouette 10 miles off, Buachaille Etive Mor made a symmetrical background with the slightly nearer bulk of Meall a' Bhuiridh, across the notch of Glen Etive.

It was behind these hills, at about 6am, that we watched the moon go down. Till the last segment vanished, its light competed with the early sun and it was impossible not to feel grateful for the bountiful service it had given us all through the night. If it had failed us and bad weather had supervened, our journey would almost certainly have had to be abandoned.

We got up without enthusiasm. We were feeling stiff and chilled, and we could not help turning a rather hostile eye on the dinghy, slumped sloppily by the edge of the loch in its dry dock of boulders. For the moment at least it had become the author of all our discomfort. Boating on remote Highland lochs seemed a sport of singularly little charm.

However, after some sandwiches and chocolate, our morale improved slightly and we even summoned up sufficient energy to pump a little air into the dinghy. It seemed particularly slow to respond and when we pushed off, just before seven o'clock, it still felt more like a suet dumpling than we might have wished.

It was a lovely morning with a true autumn hint of frosts in store. The sun was slow to reach us, skulking behind thin cloud even after it was fully up. We watched it impatiently as we plied our dripping paddles and looked with envy at the western hillside which was already warmly patterned. What mist there was lay right down on the loch,

Happy landing on the Loch Laidon beach.

rising gently from the water like steam. Its eddies filled the bays and blurred the outline of the shore, leaving only a few thin banks trailing farther out. Now and again we could hear stags roaring and over the moor we watched small herds of deer on the move. Grouse were about in plenty too, taking wing from the heather with harsh scolding. One old fellow, perched cockily on a tussock, made an unusual landmark for us as we worked our way quietly past.

After a short time we began to notice a rather sinister hissing sound which seemed to be issuing from one of the dinghy's inlet valves. Neither of us liked to mention this at first and we went paddling on stolidly, doing our best to make believe that we were concentrating on the scenery. It was a little disconcerting all the same just to sit waiting and listening, wondering the while if one final outrush of air would sink us like a stone in a grand gurgle of bubbles. In fact, it seemed rather foolish. So in the end we gave way and switched course, nose to shore, beaching finally on a small rocky headland. The trouble turned out to be what we had suspected and it took us no more than a few minutes to put it right, with a little honest pumping and some manipulation of our cork and rubber bungs. This was the one and only defect encountered in the dinghy; otherwise our confidence in it was complete.

Meanwhile, just to plague us, a breeze had begun to blow up the loch. There was little strength in it and certainly no malice, but we were glad all the same to have put Loch Laidon's first miles so well and truly behind us. The pause on the headland to mend the valve had been a welcome break in the monotony, but now as the water wrinkled ahead of us, our paddles felt suddenly heavier and our pace grew slower; solitary trees on the loch-side, by which we could measure our onward creep, took aeons of time to approach and pass and fall astern; instead of being thoroughly grateful for the sunlight now flooding about us, we took its joyful warmth for granted. Without a doubt we were beginning to look forward to taking life easy again.

Then, at last, we were able to make out familiar details beyond the head of the loch: the dark smudge of Rannoch station and close beside it the more prominent landmark of the long railway viaduct. As we looked, the smoke of a train mushroomed upwards and drifted slowly down wind. Instinctively we glanced at our watches. But there was no need for panic. This was only the early train northbound from Glasgow to Fort William; there was still plenty of time before ours, heading south, was due.

As we started on the loch's last mile, our spirits rose again. Straight ahead was our final objective, the sickle of golden beach that stood for the end of all our striving and toil. With mounting excitement we watched it drawing steadily nearer.

On our right a long headland topped with a single pine tree reached out towards the middle of the loch and we surmised that in the recess beyond it lay concealed the outflow of the River Gaur. With more time to spare we should have liked to fit in a morning's reconnaissance, exploring this corner where the river has its birth and starts on its lively descent towards Bridge of Gaur. If only it were navigable, what a superb link it would make in the obvious sequel to our Rannoch crossing! Down to Loch Rannoch itself, then on to the challenge of Tummel and Tay; some day it might be that we would return and try out possibilities for ourselves.

We altered course slightly to port, paddling close in under the heather-crowned banks of the northern shore and aiming eventually for the nearest corner of the beach. Up on the slopes above we could pick out the kinks and switchbacks of the track which runs parallel to the water's edge and which clearly makes pleasant going hereabouts. Two hikers off the morning train, weighed down by enormous rucksacks and heading westwards for the moor, were making their way along it. As they came level with us they gave us a wave and a cheery shout.

A hundred yards – 50 – 20 – 10 – steadily the gap narrowed. Then quite suddenly the dinghy was crunching on small shingle, gently-angled. It slid to a stop and we sat back, laying aside our dripping paddles. I turned to face Lindley, smiling broadly beneath the expansive brim of the shako. Then I shook him by the hand; it was, I reckoned, a suitably solemn occasion.

After a little we stood up and stepped ashore, tugging at the dinghy till it was high and dry beside us on the beach. And so, quietly and undramatically, the journey ended. Everything had gone according to plan. The weather had been kind to us; the dinghy had maintained its high standard of reliability; the last miles of Loch Laidon had not, after all, turned into a wild race against the clock. As my thoughts went jerkily over the rather odd

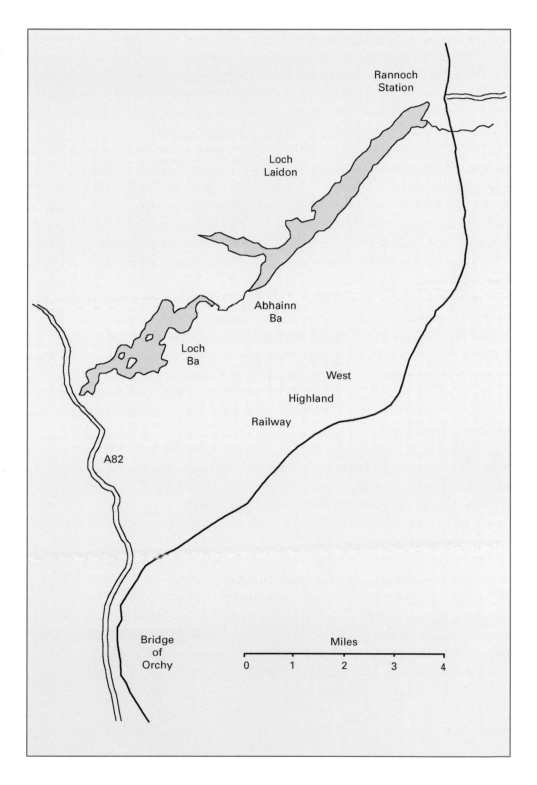

Rannoch
Station

Loch
Laidon

Abhainn
Ba

Loch
Ba

West

Highland

Railway

A82

Bridge
of
Orchy

Miles

0   1   2   3   4

sequence of events from the idea's birth to the actuality of our final exhilarating touch-down, my satisfaction could not have been more complete.

We deflated the dinghy and stuffed it unceremoniously into its canvas container along with the rest of our gear. Then, with the whole thing suspended from the paddles, we laid these on our shoulders and set off along the path to Rannoch station. Behind us Loch Laidon was mirror calm, for the breeze had fallen away again. Even so it was not too difficult to imagine the tribulation we might have had to endure, had the weather kicked up really rough. The track we were now treading so peacefully might well have seemed a very long way indeed.

We reached the station in good order and soon were in the throes of sorting out the bewildering muddle of our kit. This done, we tackled the more serious business of second breakfast and even managed to take some thought to our appearances. Then the train came clanking in and we hoisted ourselves and the gear aboard into an unpopular huddle in the corridor.

Barely an hour later we were back at our old 'advanced base' close beside Loch Ba.

The return journey had been accomplished absurdly quickly. Indeed it had been almost depressing to watch from the train windows how the miles of the moor slipped past. Loch Laidon a brief last glint of silver; the brown slopes of Beinn Creachan; the pines of the old Wood of Crannach – one picture had followed the other in close sequence, like the spinning of a well-known film in reverse. Maybe, having sampled these few minutes of superficial viewing, we could value the more what we had gained from our own painstaking creep to the east.

Now, as we stood at the roadside beside the parked car, we let time slow down once again. It was a lovely September morning. Over the patchwork browns and yellows of Rannoch Moor the sun streamed free, while up on Stob Ghabhar the long ridges seemed to crown with a halo of light the dark recesses of the corries.

We strolled over toward the edge of the loch and gazed idly across its quiet blue water. Automatically our thoughts went back over the events of the past sixteen hours, the experiences we had had since first we started puzzling out our island-dodging in the moonlight. Now the adventure was over. There was nothing more to it except the prosaic drive back to the city.

But as I turned to the final task of loading up the car I realised that whatever sailing I might happen to do in days to come, I would always think with very special gratitude of the dinghy and the trips it had made possible. As the Tar remarked of the Vital Spark: 'I've seen a wheen o' vessels since I left her, but none that had her style nor nicer shupmates.'

Chapter Thirteen

TWICE TOLD TALES 2
– ULVA, 1963

I N an immense ragged crescent, the west coast of the island of Mull sweeps round from Calgary Bay in the north to the Ross of Mull and Iona in the south. Half way across the entrance, like a string of beads, stretch the Treshnish Isles – Carn a' Burg Mor and Carn a' Burg Beag, Fladda, Lunga and the Dutchman's Cap. Inside cluster another half dozen islands – Ulva and Gometra, Eorsa and Inchkenneth, Little Colonsay and Staffa, each with its attendant outliers. Backed by lonely cliffs and hills, the archipelago makes one of the most fascinating sections of the whole Scottish coastline.

Twice – in August 1943 and in May 1946 – I had the good fortune to look down on the islands; raven's eye views from the summit cairn of Ben More, highest of the Mull hills. This double introduction was followed not long afterwards by two unsuccessful attempts to reach Staffa and first acquaintance instead with Iona, but it was not until 1963 that I managed to carry out a plan which had been clamouring for attention for some time: the paying of a quick visit to Ulva, largest of these satellite islands of Mull.

Leisure unfortunately was limited. A single day was all that could be spared, a fact which posed something of a problem, as it was still the summer before the introduction of the island car-ferries. There was one outward passenger sailing from Oban to Mull at nine o'clock every morning, but it was only on Thursday evenings that the MacBrayne timetable conceded a late steamer back from Tobermory to Oban. Just once a week, then, there was the chance to enjoy a really full day on Mull and beyond.

I left Glasgow by car at six o'clock on a perfect June morning. The radiance of the early sunshine quickly wiped out the memory of jangling alarm-clock and scanty breakfast. Up Loch Lomondside into Glen Falloch, through the suntrap of Glen Lochy, down beside the umber and yellow tide-wrack of Loch Etive the heat grew steadily. And there, reaching to horizons already vague in haze, lay the Firth of Lorne still and untroubled under a brazen sky.

The *King George V* slipped out of Oban Bay to meet only the laziest of swells. Even off Lady Rock the tide-jabble could barely be felt as we passed between it and Lismore into the mirror calm of the Sound of Mull. As I disembarked at Tobermory and watched the *King George V* swing away again from the pier to continue her run north-about round Mull to Staffa and Iona, it was impossible not to feel envious of the passengers still on board. The thought of the day of ease which lay before them made any kind of effort ashore seem singularly unattractive by comparison.

Main Street, Tobermory, gave back the heat like the inner lining of a baking-tin. Here and there above the roadway the air was beginning to dance and shimmer in mirage-pools of quicksilver. Already the day promised to break all previous records of a sweltering midsummer week.

Unfortunately the day's work had to start sometime. Shouldering my pessimistically heavy rucksack, I set off to claim the bicycle which I had previously arranged to hire for the day.

My expectations could not have been said to be high: cycling on Mull has always seemed to me to plumb depths of wretchedness utterly unknown elsewhere. I proceeded to the back of the shop in the wake of the owner much as one might have accepted an invitation to inspect the tumbril that was to transport one to the guillotine.

'Where are you bound for?' asked my companion brightly, producing the machine on which the day's destiny was to hang. I noticed with some satisfaction that it had the traditional two wheels and handlebars, also a saddle of sorts. No doubt the snags would show themselves later on.

'Dervaig,' I replied, 'then, if possible, over to Ulva. Why?' A momentary shadow seemed to have crossed his face.

'Nothing really. I was only wondering if you knew the Dervaig road. The hills on it, I mean. They're worth treating with a bit of respect, you know. Just the other day there we had a couple of girl visitors from Dervaig on their bicycles and one of them went over the handlebars and stunned herself.'

I commiserated rather wanly. A certain amount of pessimism, it seemed, was warranted.

To begin with, however, there was little actual danger: it was impossible to cycle at all. The road climbed steeply, interminably, upwards, at first shut in, but twisting higher through the outskirts of the town. All one could do was trudge slowly uphill, yard after dusty yard; it seemed a mere mockery to have to push a bicycle as well. Then at length the trees thinned and the last of the houses was left behind. The air freshened, the outlook widened, and the road, after a final defiant lift, began to level off more charitably. Clearly the time had come to mount; there was nothing for it but to grit the teeth and get on with it, like Macbeth:

'I am settled, and bend up each corporal agent to this terrible feat.'

The first part of the journey – the seven-mile stretch to Dervaig – was not slow to demand attention. In particular it was necessary to re-learn the old lesson that suddenly having to start pedalling a bicycle after years of abstinence and without any previous training is a good deal less pleasant than facing the same bit of road from behind the steering wheel of a car.

Not that there was any excuse for grumbling, certainly not so far as weather and views were concerned. It was a peerless morning, still young and fresh, and bright with the exhilaration of June at its best. Larks and meadow pipits exulted in an outpouring of song, accompanied rather less musically by the restless chacking of wheatears and an occasional stonechat. The sun even seemed to have drawn from the surrounding moorland a double measure of that heady compound of scents, so completely indefinable and essentially Highland – bog myrtle and young heather and invading bracken shoots.

The narrow, curving Mishnish Lochs, which border the road for close on two miles, had a royalty in their blueness that I had forgotten existed anywhere south of Sutherland. So brilliant, too, was the green of their banks that the sudden vividness of colouring was almost startling. From a white shingle spit a pair of sandpipers took flight, piping anxiously as they skimmed the loch-fringe. Here the going was more level and much pleasanter in consequence. Indeed almost before I had realised it, I had reached the far end. This was fully half way to Dervaig and an excellent excuse for a halt, so I dismounted and sat back luxuriously, shoulders propped against a dusty bank where thyme and ling sprawled.

The chain of the three Mishnish Lochs lies at an altitude of almost 500 feet and it is from the west end of their moorland saucer that the road takes its first plunge. It seemed a delightful change, of course, to be starting to freewheel at last, but in less than 100 yards it became alarmingly clear that this was no more than an irony of fate: quite suddenly the gradient was so fierce, the surface so loose, the cornering so violent, that I had to clutch wildly at the brakes, hoping fervently that I might escape being pitched head over handlebars into the heather. On and on wound the descent, bend after loose gritty bend, and on and on we bounced and juddered, the machine and I, brakes grating, teeth rattling, till I wondered if there would ever be any end to it all. Just when I was almost resigned to letting go and having one last dramatic gamble with gravity, the angle eased to a level stretch and it was possible to draw breath more normally. Death by stunning, swift, spectacular and final, had been avoided after all.

Having dropped the best part of 300 feet, the road flattened momentarily beside the head of little Loch an Torr. From a nearby bed of reeds a heron flew off, abandoning its morning fishing. Its slow, leisurely wing-beats seemed almost a reproof – a condemnation of every kind of haste and impatience and unnecessary work.

The bicycle and I eventually reached Dervaig a few minutes before midday, sustained by nothing other than the sheer perfection of the morning. We had mastered a second, seemingly endless ascent, a series of hairpin bends tilted wickedly upwards, and we had swooped and swung down the further side, the aerial views of the village a reassurance that the first part of the journey was coming to a successful conclusion. Seven hot miles lay behind and we were still up to schedule.

There was, that June morning, something about Dervaig itself reminiscent of one of the villages of the Austrian Tyrol. The dusty white road dropping into it with such abruptness might well have been the descent from some high altitude pass. Its clustered houses and gardens gave a first impression of peace and timelessness. With the feeling of a hard morning's work well done, my spirits were high as I went pedalling through. Soon now the first views of Mull's west coast would be coming up. Everything seemed combined in such perfection that I was very nearly tempted to risk a stave or two of one of the more popular songs. Benignly I smiled on a local heifer that raised an eyebrow at my passing from the far side of a fence.

Then suddenly, without warning, misfortune struck.

The bicycle juddered over a more ragged pothole than usual and a moment later the front tyre had gone soft as pulp. We slowed to an anxious halt.

Now, of all the practical tasks at which I am almost uncannily useless the mending of bicycle punctures must surely top the list. Here, if anywhere, is an inescapable personal Waterloo. This was no exception. The preliminary ritual of disembowelment having been carried through, it was discovered as usual that the inner tube was scarred and mottled with a rash of patches as though sorely stricken with measles. There being no obvious hole, however, a bowl of water was borrowed from a sympathetic housewife and the partially inflated tube immersed. Nothing moved. Not a bubble rose from the crystal depths of the water. It was left entirely to the imagination to guess which of the spots looked thinnest. Then, the most likely having been selected and patched, the tyre was reassembled and put to the test.

If possible, it was flatter than before.

An hour and three-quarters later I found myself sitting back luxuriously in one of Dervaig's two taxis, climbing the rutted short-cut that curls over the hill to Torloisk. Much valuable time had been squandered before this happy state of affairs had been achieved, but now all the necessary arrangements had been completed. I had eaten my lunch and had even made big efforts to curb my impatience. The bicycle was out of sight and almost out of mind, safe in the keeping of the village blacksmith, whose nonchalant attitude to puncture-mending was one to inspire the deepest admiration. The machine, he assured me, would be ready waiting on my return later in the afternoon. It was possible to face the future again with a certain amount of optimism.

Quite suddenly, just past the watershed of our hill-road, the islands came into view: Ulva and Gometra straight ahead, their humped black masses surprisingly close and, against the sun, magnified unnaturally by the surrounding dazzle of light; out to sea the main chain of Treshnish – Fladda, Lunga, the Dutchman's Cap – islands that are impossible to glimpse without a catch at the breath. There they were again, inviting, alluring, tantalising, withdrawn in the grey distance of the heat-haze. Even if the day were to bring no further satisfaction, the toil that lay behind would not have been in vain. This panorama of well-known islands, as much perhaps as Ulva itself, was what I had come to enjoy.

Not far from the junction of our track with the main road we passed Torloisk House. Unobtrusive behind screening trees, its name only just distinguishable on the half-inch map, Torloisk is nevertheless a place of great interest. Before the days of steamboats, it shared with Ulva the honour of being one of the jumping-off points for visitors to Staffa. Towards the end of the 18th century such a trip was quite an undertaking. First one had to travel by fishing-smack from Oban to Aros, in Mull; then there was a walk, or more likely a ride on Highland pony-back, across the island to Torloisk or Ulva Ferry; finally, when the weather deigned to permit, there was the crossing by sailing boat of nine miles of open sea. Small wonder if the whole expedition sometimes took as long as ten days or a fortnight to accomplish.

It was from Torloisk that the famous French geologist and traveller, Faujas de Saint Fond, sailed out on his visit to Staffa in 1784, 12 years after the island's 'discovery' by Sir Joseph Banks. Saint Fond must have set off with a good deal of misgiving, for some of the other members of his party, eight in all with one day's provisions, had already been out to the island and had actually been storm-bound there for two days, living in incredible squalor with the local inhabitants – 16 men, women and children, eight cows, one bull, 12 sheep, two horses, one pig, two dogs, one cock and eight hens. It is not recorded how far the livestock population was reduced in order to alleviate the visitors' pangs of hunger. For Saint Fond himself the sea was calmer and after a pleasantly full day on the island, the return to Torloisk was made in four and a half hours.

It was a pleasant five miles from Torloisk to the Ulva ferry. After the short-cut over the moors the road seemed reasonable and sedate, its bordering trees remarkably profuse. Here and there hoodie crows were busy among the rocks and seaweed and once, briefly, we glimpsed a fine waterfall, the Eas Fors, tumbling white down a deep black scimitar-gash in the cliffs. In due course I was disgorged at the ferry, the taxi-driver agreeing to return for me again at 5.30pm. Thanks to the puncture the time allowance for Ulva had been cut to a miserable fraction.

At the top of the slipway an enormous grocer's van was parked, its driver busy inside amid a bewilderment of stores. Close by the ferryman's wife was sitting enjoying the sunshine.

'Just over doing the shopping,' she remarked cheerfully as I shed my rucksack and took a seat on the concrete parapet. 'My husband's across at the house but he'll be back on this side in a few minutes. I take it you're wanting over.' I admitted that that was my intention, then told how my time had been whittled down by ill luck. 'And that, I'm afraid, puts paid to reaching Gometra too. I'm hoping all the same to have a look at the basaltic columns on Ulva; can you tell me the best way over to them?'

'Well, you won't want to waste any time. It's quite a distance. My husband will be able to tell you the road to take.'

And so in due course he did, most helpfully, as we sat in the big broad-beamed ferry-boat, luxuriating in the warmth and watching the green water of the sound slipping quietly astern.

It is only some 200 yards from Mull across to Ulva; a sea-lane that is trifling, insignificant – and thoroughly deceptive. Through its jaws and over its submerged reefs spin the tides between Loch Tuath and Loch na Keal; 'a narrow intricate channel with many dangers' runs the official Admiralty description. Yet as we saw it nothing could have looked more innocent. Scarcely a ripple furrowed the water, smooth, cool, tempting. The sail was no more than a few minutes' further relaxation before work began again.

It was amusing to recall some of the illustrious travellers of the past who in their day had made this same island crossing. Boswell and Johnson, huddled in their cloaks against the harsh wind, making the passage in the longboat of the Irish vessel *Bonnetta* on a pitch-black night of mid-October 1773. 'It was the sixteenth of October,' commented Johnson, 'a time when it is not convenient to sleep in the Hebrides without a cover.' James Hogg, the Ettrick Shepherd, visiting Staffa and Fingal's Cave and complaining in visitors' book doggerel of the greed of the local boatmen. Sir Walter Scott, outward bound on the first of his two visits to Staffa, crossing to Ulva with 'colours flying and pipes playing' on a bright July day in 1810. He was to be the guest of the laird, Ranald MacDonald, and came ashore to a princely welcome accompanied by discharges of musketry and artillery.

My own landing had less obvious pomp and ceremony. As I shouldered my rucksack and walked off the slipway, the island seemed deserted, as lacking in interest in my arrival as the few idling gulls. The shore, the beginnings of a road, even the ferryman's cottage had apparently succumbed to the tyranny of afternoon heat. The only sound of any kind was the diminishing throb of the engine as the ferry-boat recrossed the narrows to Mull.

With the rather forlorn hope of reaching Ulva's highest point, Beinn Chreagach (1,025ft), I set off along the rough white road, its surface parched and dusty. At first it led across fairly open country, edged by clusters of foxgloves and flag irises. At one or two of the corners and forks, signposts pointed bleached wooden fingers to show the way to Gometra. Then followed a wooded stretch, thick higher up with larches and firs, and noisy at one point with the screeching and chatter of a heronry. I could have wished for the shade to last longer than it did for a little more help in maintaining a fast pace. But there was no justice: instead of rewarding honest toil the wood ended abruptly, giving place to open moorland where the sun at once resumed its merciless oppression. This was the butterfly zone, dozens of fritillaries and an occasional small tortoiseshell dancing ahead over the heather, while the number of blues I saw suggested the coast of Fife rather than Argyll. And again, most noticeably, there was the nostalgic scent of bog myrtle and ling.

The summit of Beinn Chreagach – if indeed it really was the summit that was visible

Ulva. The ferryman arrives to take me across.

– looked several miles away in the haze. It crowned ring upon ring of rounded basalt terraces, the whole formation, according to one guidebook writer, resembling the pyramids. Somewhere beyond lay Gometra. With more time available it would have been quite accessible, especially as a bridge spans the Bru, the narrow strait which separates it from Ulva. But even under ideal conditions such an addition to the programme would have meant a most strenuous afternoon; with the temperature soaring as it was, I was unashamedly glad it was out of the question.

There was no point therefore in following the road further, so I turned off on to the open hillside, making height steadily by a succession of helpful paths. Gradually the views opened out – on the one hand Loch Tuath, with its Mull background marked noticeably by the white scar of the Eas Fors; on the other the scattering of the seaward islands, growing every moment into a more complicated design. And, behind, always the half-distinguishable mass of Ben More.

Quite soon it became obvious that there was no hope even for the last half mile to the top of Beinn Chreagach. With a detour to the south shore still in prospect, the two miles already covered in considerable haste had been effort enough. I dumped my rucksack therefore and sat down to confront a jam roll, squashed, sticky and completely delectable. Sadly there was no time to spare for a real siesta to match.

My way from the hog's back of Beinn Chreagach down to the south shore cut tiresomely across the line of the gullies. Moreover, Ulva is notorious for the prolific growth of its bracken – it is said to grow in places to heights which can easily hide all but the horns of the Highland cattle – and although it was too early in the summer for quite such luxuriance, I had to wallow and flounder often enough. On the airless lower ground, hurrying past the crumbled skeletons of old cottages overgrown with thistles and nettles and masses of buttercups, I grew hotter and hotter still. There was always the hope of finding a burn and this acted as a constant spur, but not a trickle was to be seen anywhere; each likely hollow in turn was parched and thirsty as my throat, and even when I reached the sea's edge at last there was no consolation, as time was now too short for a swim.

It was not far along the shore to the first of the basaltic outcrops – a low cliff, brown and wrinkled as a centenarian's face and brightly coloured at its base with clumps of bell heather. Beyond, on the farther arm of a small bay, stood two imposing rock-towers.

Dr John Macculloch, that extraordinarily enterprising and energetic traveller who roamed the Highlands and islands in the days of the Prince Regent, commented aptly:

> On the south-western shore of Ulva, the columnar rocks are often disposed in a very picturesque manner; being often broken, sometimes detached, and occasionally bearing a distant resemblance to ruined walls and towers. Had Ulva been the only basaltic island on this coast, it might possibly have attracted more attention; but it has been eclipsed by Staffa, and has remained unsung.

A stone's throw beyond was a shallow grotto, lines of basalt pillars resting like organ-pipes on the wide arch of its roof. It was farther still, however, that I came on the best architecture of all: a small pebbled cove hemmed in by a high columnar wall. Here the pillars stood tall and regular, austerely straight and matched precisely for size. At the tip of the promontory they plunged, knife-edged, into the blue-green of the sea, a patch of white surf ringing their base. Comparisons with Staffa or the Shiant Isles would be profitless, yet in their own way, with their warm brown texture and capping of green grass set against the expanse of the sea and the background cliffs of Gribun, these fine columns made an impression that was quite remarkably vivid.

Time had moved swiftly since the pause up on the shoulder of Beinn Chreagach; Ulva's jealously reckoned ration of hours and minutes was almost at an end. It would have been pleasant to turn a few more corners of coastline, but now the temptation had to be resisted. There was no choice but to strike straight back to the ferry.

A herd of Highland cattle, gold and brown and absurdly shaggy for the day before midsummer, eyed me askance as I dived afresh into the bracken and started to struggle uphill once again. Immediately the green fronds clutched affectionately at my ankles, and every boulder and hole on the hillside seemed to have aligned itself directly in my path. Clearly it was to be a strenuous race against time.

Columnar basalt pillar on the south-west shore of Ulva.

A formal burial place, prominent on the top of a high hillock, would ordinarily have invited a visit, but now it had to be passed strongmindedly by. It was only possible to conjecture who lay buried there: some of the Clan MacQuarrie, maybe, whose ownership of Ulva is said to have lasted for 900 years; or possibly some of the MacArthurs, at one time famous for the college of piping which they conducted on the island. Whoever they may have been, the people who were brought here, they were given a matchless site for their last resting-place.

Not far beyond, Ulva House itself barred the way and called for a suitable detour, behind a screen of rhododendrons then through a hostile tangle of undergrowth. It was a relief to reach the road again and face the last dusty half mile to the ferry. On the far side of the sound I could see the car already waiting.

The outstanding event of the drive back to Dervaig was undoubtedly our stop at the schoolhouse. Here the kind lady who opened the door must surely have caught the glint of urgency in my eye, for without wasting time she hustled me through to the kitchen tap. Then, with growing incredulity, she watched while I made up for the aridity of Ulva. It was a moment when I would undoubtedly have subscribed to Para Handy's theory that 'long life iss aal a maitter o' moisture.'

As I relaxed in the taxi once again and watched the miles slipping by, I could not avoid a certain sneaking hope, faint it is true, but unworthy none the less – the hope that the Dervaig blacksmith had not been able to mend the puncture. If this were so then, of course, it would be possible to travel back in luxury and with a completely clear conscience the whole way to Tobermory, while the wretched bicycle was left to follow on by lorry the following morning. It was an agreeable speculation.

Unfortunately no sooner had we reached Dervaig Hotel than the hope was utterly shattered. There, propped up against the wall, was the machine itself, looking disgustingly fit, its tyres fairly exuding good health and vitality. Not the flimsiest excuse was left.

In the end the seven miles to Tobermory took little more than an hour. They even had my spirits soaring again, for they finished in the exhilaration of a descent that was of just the right steepness and manageably smooth. As I dismounted and wheeled the machine into its stable, I felt more than ordinarily content.

It was a perfect evening. The gold of the sun's rays, low-slanting now, struck across the blue of the bay to the barrier of Calve Island. The haze had gone; there was not a cloud in the sky; every colour glittered with a breath-taking clarity. Main Street was noisy with talk and laughter, almost as if everyone sensed the blessing of this incomparable June sundown.

Sailing-time was officially 8pm, but it was later than that before the masts of the *Lochnevis*, disembodied by the intervening segment of Calve Island, could be seen moving ghost-like up the Sound of Mull. The passengers on board were on an evening cruise from Oban and it was a cheery throng that lined the rails as the steamer manoeuvred to the pier.

The call was brief, the engine-room telegraph jangling impatiently when we swung away once more. Soon Tobermory was lost to sight as we turned down the Sound.

Toward the west the sky flamed with the sunset, dazzlingly bright, the steamer's wake making an unbroken avenue of gold into the very heart of the fire. Against the brilliance I watched the tireless retinue of gulls, endlessly planing and swaying to the air currents.

Over the Mull hills the white heat was beginning to cool and later, far down the Firth of Lorne, the Isles of the Sea were merging into the dove-grey of early twilight. Oban gave us due welcome and as I drove the last 90-mile lap back home to Glasgow, the radiance of the afterglow picked out one after another the silhouettes of familiar hills.

Chapter Fourteen

TWICE TOLD TALES 3
– OVER THE TOPS, 1958

Up in the north-east it had been a particularly hard winter. Blizzard after blizzard had swept the high ground, piling the snow-beds in the corries to immense depths and leaving few bald patches on the upper ridges. Even at lower levels in Banffshire and Aberdeenshire the snowploughs had been heavily overworked and almost as far down as the Moray coast roadside drifts and white fields had come to be accepted as normal.

There was, in short, no excuse. The time had come to remove the rust and dust from my equipment and realise an ambition of long standing – one of those ambitions that have a particularly strong appeal when considered from the depths of an armchair – a crossing of the Cairngorms on skis.

The only brief moments of glory to brighten the drabness of my career as a skier had come during my short wartime spell in Chamonix with the 5th Scots Guards. After this meteor-flash of brilliance obscurity had supervened once more. Indeed in all likelihood there would never have been anything further to add, had it not been for my friend Theo Nicholson.

Almost always on our numerous hill-days together Theo and I would talk over future ploys. One of these had been a plan for a long day on skis, well away from the crowds and of course as we pictured it, with snow and weather conditions at their idyllic best. It was quite early on that I had ventured to suggest a crossing of the Cairngorms.

The most remarkable thing about this idea was that Theo should ever have given it a second thought. His skiing experience was immense, ranging from the Canadian Rockies through Britain and most of the Alps to the farthest corners of Scandinavia, and the prospect of crawling across the plateau of the Cairngorms in company with a particularly lame duck can only have filled him with dismay. However, even after a day on Meall a' Bhuiridh, in Glencoe, when he had ample opportunity to see me at my worst, he still managed to say he thought the scheme was a good one. This, I decided, was chivalry at its finest.

Eventually we managed to get down to actual planning, noting with a good deal of alarm how quickly the expedition seemed to assume the appearance of a full-scale military operation.

The route itself was soon agreed on. From the Linn of Dee, six miles from Braemar, it would lie west then north-west to take in three summits, all of which at that time would be new to me at least – Carn Cloich-mhuillin (3,087ft), Beinn Bhrotain (3,795ft) and Monadh Mor (3,651ft); it would then cross the expanse of the Great Moss and, cutting over the shoulder of Carn Ban Mor (3,443ft) not far south of the cairn, would drop finally to Achlean farm in Glen Feshie. The total distance would be some 20 miles and there would be rather more than 3,500 feet of climbing.

These details were perfectly simple. There were, however, complications of our own making, for we debated whether, if weather conditions were unfavourable, it might not be advisable to do the crossing in the reverse direction – roughly north-south instead of south-north. This introduced a new element into our planning which was not at all helpful, and before we knew quite what had happened we found ourselves in a mist of uncertainty. Long-range forecasts, highs and lows over Greenland or Scandinavia, probable and improbable snow conditions – the more we thought about what we might meet, the more unsettling it all became. We took our problem to the met office men and they could not have tried to be more helpful, but they were also extremely cautious in their more distant forecasting and it was clear that in the last resort the success of the project must depend on our own judgment and what the day itself brought forth.

At times, too, the make-up of the party seemed to be as variable as the weather itself. Several friends were keen to come with us, but it was quite impossible to find dates to suit everyone and in the end all that was left was a quartet of age and youth: Theo and his son John, a friend of the latter, Robert Dean, and myself. The awkward problem of transport was happily solved when Theo's wife Thelma generously volunteered to drive round the hundred miles between start and finish, hopefully to carry us back in due course to the fleshpots.

Gradually all the various details were settled, and when at last the met office ventured a more confident prediction of a spell of cold, bright March weather with winds light to moderate veering north-east, we actually went so far as to name the day. Our initial south-north choice, Deeside to Speyside, seemed the more sensible direction after all, with the Cairngorm Club hut at Muir of Inverey near Braemar an obviously excellent starting-point. There was no longer any hope of a reprieve.

Or, as my daughter happily put it: 'It'll be a wonderful trip to describe, Dad. If you survive.'

As we turned off the road to the cottage at Muir of Inverey, the sun was already setting in frosty splendour. It had been a day of no wind and remarkably little cloud, and as we drove north through the length of Perthshire and into Aberdeenshire, our spirits had been justifiably high. On the familiar hills flanking the road over the Cairnwell the sparkling snowfields and well-filled corries had given promise of great things for the morrow. For Theo perhaps, with his ample experience of cross-country travel in Norway, it would be a day of negligible significance, but so far as I was concerned it was to be an introduction to mountain touring on a bigger scale than I had known before, to the one side of skiing which had always had outstanding appeal. The long, clear views had seemed somehow prophetic; now, more prosaically, as we busied ourselves unloading the car, opening up the cottage and fetching pine logs for the stove, we could feel the sudden bitterness of the frost. Ears and fingertips were quickly chilled and in the keen air the least sound carried far.

There is nothing at all spartan about the Muir of Inverey cottage-hut. Once the coal and pine log stove is well alight, the spacious kitchen-living room becomes a place of real comfort. An electric cooker, a hot water immerser and well-equipped cupboards make cooking simple, while in the dormitories there are even heaters available in case taking to one's bunk should be altogether too chilly to endure.

We spent the evening in a genial fug at the stove, doing our best to digest a culinary masterpiece of Theo's which could only have been described as a horsey hoosh. Then, not reluctantly, we yawned our way off to bed.

Next morning there was a scattering of cloud about, but it had done nothing to lessen the intense cold, and we agreed that it looked certain to clear later. Theo had whipped us into a shuffle of activity around 5.30am, but a further hour and a half had gone by before we were finished with breakfast and had loaded the car with our equipment. Unashamedly we were driven to the Linn of Dee, one valuable mile on our way.

This was not, of course, a luxury which could be spun out at all; in less than five minutes we were piling out again under the pines. Before us stretched the track to White Bridge, unusable by car by reason of the padlocked gate which barred the way.

It was a delightful walk of 55 minutes. The road had an honest sandy surface and at first we felt out of luck that we had not been able to obtain permission to use the car; farther on, however, we changed our tune, for increasingly numerous snowdrifts, iron hard, presented obstacles that would obviously have caused a great deal of trouble. In any case it was much too enjoyable an introduction for us to have the least regrets. It was good just to be alive on such a morning. The air was keen, heady, exhilarating, our pace nicely judged to warm us to the day's work. Close to the track we saw several small parties of stags and hinds, their colouring blending closely with the tawny-browns of the hillsides. Down by the Dee, where occasionally ice floes drifted past, oystercatchers went piping over the shingle-spits, while now and again a grouse whirred clacking from the heather – cheerful reminders of the birdsong we might have been enjoying hereabouts, had this been May or June.

Of the higher hills we had poor views: nothing more interesting than those humps beside the upper Geldie, Carn Ealar and An Sgarsoch. But after a couple of miles the dull moors on our right fell back and there, quite suddenly, was our shapely first top, Carn

The long snow-slope leading to the top of Beinn Bhrotain.

Cloich-mhuillin, with a great white billow behind it, frozen into immobility at the moment of breaking – the summit crest of Beinn Bhrotain. Up there lay our route.

Situated at an altitude of 1,336 feet, White Bridge is not actually white but grey; solid wooden superstructure on solid stone piers. Just before it is reached a signpost marks the parting of the ways, one green arm pointing right, to Aviemore via the Lairig Ghru, the other across the bridge, to Glen Tilt and Glen Feshie.

We were to see something of Glen Tilt as we went on our way, now following the farther bank of the Dee on short, crisp heather. It featured prominently in our backward views, a deep trench cut below the snow-plastering of Beinn a' Ghlo and leading back, it seemed to suggest, to the warmer, friendlier country of the South.

It was not far from here, in the year 1749, that one of a detachment of English soldiers stationed near White Bridge was murdered. A few years later two Highlanders were arrested for the crime and taken to Edinburgh for trial at the High Court. The proceedings went forward with due solemnity until the chief witness for the prosecution told how he had seen and talked with the English soldier's ghost, and so learned the names of the murderers.

'And what language was it that he talked?' he was asked by the defending advocate.

'As good Gaelic as myself,' came the answer. And the case ended in unexpected mirth.

After a quarter of a mile we left the riverbank and made straight for the top of Carn Cloich-mhuillin, still almost three miles away. The going remained mostly over heather, for so far these south-facing slopes were not high enough to carry more than patches of snow. Our skis at this time, bowing us down and chafing our shoulders, seemed so much unnecessary lumber. Fortunately, however, the weather could scarcely have been kinder, with little or no wind and a mother-of-pearl sky that gave promise of even better things to come. Now opening out north-eastwards, the gateway to the Lairig – on the one side the Devil's Point and on the other Carn a' Mhaim – had all the impressive grandeur of a high Alpine pass.

The sun burst through as we approached the top of Carn Cloich-mhuillin, performing with sudden generosity a miracle of colour transformation. In the granite of the boulders and screes we discovered shell-pink and coral and sandy-brown; in the lichens, yellows and greens and greys. New brightness swept across the moors below, and against the spreading blue above, the upper snowfields of Beinn Bhrotain and Ben Macdhui stretched long arcs of silver.

We were thankful all the same for a lazy quarter of an hour at the cairn. We lay back satisfied and enjoyed the far views: Lochnagar and the Ben Uarns, the Blair Atholl hills, Ben Alder and Creag Meaghaidh, possibly even Ben Nevis in the distant jumble of Lochaber. We looked down too on the headwaters of the Feshie and the Geldie, running almost parallel within a stone's throw of each other, yet the one flowing to the Spey, the other to the Dee. This bleak bit of moorland must surely be quite the loneliest stretch of the Aberdeenshire-Inverness-shire border; how soon, I wondered, would it be traversed by a road that would bring Speyside within easy reach of Deeside, a road that would fulfil the dream of General Wade more than two centuries ago, to link the barracks at Ruthven, near Kingussie, with Braemar?

The time was 10.15am. We had been going now for more than three hours. And so far we had not even thought of putting on skis. I was not, however, to be allowed to escape for much longer. At the saddle beyond Carn Cloich-mhuillin – after a stepped descent that suggested to me the side of the Great Pyramid of Cheops – we reached snow at last, its surface hard, deep, unbroken.

I unfastened my skis from the sling around my neck, fitted them with skins and bent to clip them on. Then, very gingerly, I started to straighten up. On the way I seemed to sway like a ship at sea and had to lean desperately on my sticks. I glanced at the others; they were chatting away happily, completely unaware of this moment of anguish. Then at last I was vertical and could draw breath. It would have been inauspicious to fall flat on my back before we had even started.

From the col it was a continuous snow-slope all the way to the top of Beinn Bhrotain; a delightful climb, sun-warmed and exhilarating. Much of the crust was heavily iced and at one point early on our skis cut tramlines across the surface of a frozen lochan. Beyond this the angle steepened sharply and we took a long diagonal, so long that I reckoned these must certainly be the eternal snows. It was difficult not to envy Theo's easy-looking style, long stride and powerful forward thrust combined in a perfection of rhythm obviously acquired under Norwegian masters. Every time a ski went forward, whether on the level or moving uphill, he would gain a few inches; not much, but always inexorably, something. The result was that very soon he – and John with him – were far in the lead. Toiling along in their wake, I felt unpleasantly like the losing crew in the Boat Race. The only consolation was that for most of the way I had Robert's company. He had no skins for his skis and in consequence had to endure the penance of a long and wearisome carry. As he and I reached the fringe of rocks at the summit plateau, a covey of ptarmigan took off, a sudden whirr of grey and white wings. Then, thankfully, we were at the twin cairns, the second a well built wall rather than a cairn, enclosing the concrete Ordnance Survey block and providing a comfortable-looking resting-place for Theo and John.

Beinn Bhrotain (3,795ft) is the eighth highest summit of the Cairngorms; west of the Lairig only the four-thousanders Braeriach and Cairn Toul surpass it. It was also by almost 150 feet the highest point of our own day and we felt duly conscious of work well done. Of all the Cairngorms it is said to give the finest view down the Dee Valley, but I cannot honestly say I noticed it; instead I was hypnotised by our first glimpse of the real test ahead – Monadh Mor and the immense white desert of Moine Mhor, the 'great moss'. The farther rim of the latter, for which we were aiming, looked quite close, but I decided that the distance must be deceptive. Just how deceptive it was, we were to find out soon enough.

Cowardly-wise, I decided to keep the skins on my skis for the descent to the Monadh

Mor bealach. The drop was almost 600 feet and I knew it would not be gentle; anything in the way of brakes to check an uncontrolled rush was much to be desired. It was easy enough to fiddle about with my bindings to make quite sure I would be last away, at the same time sneaking a sidelong glance at the other three. Theo's judgment was masterly. He swung wide to the left, well clear of the scattering of rocks that stood out like fangs eager to snap at the first miscalculation. In beautifully controlled swings and christies he traced a route down the best of the snow until it was possible to work back on a long, straight traverse. Soon all three of them were out of sight on a bulge of steeper slopes below. My own take-off could be shirked no longer.

Fortunately it was unobserved, unless perhaps by a stray ptarmigan or two. Once under way I found the snow continuously tricky, in some places viciously iced, in others fluted and furrowed by the wind. The skins on my skis certainly checked my pace, but they made turning even more difficult than usual and I felt as ungainly as a crab on seaweed; no doubt I looked like one too. Leg muscles, strained unnaturally at each clumsy change of direction, were soon burning and aching in protest. It was only too obvious that for me the day's downhill running was to mean no respite and remarkably little pleasure. In spite of the added difficulty it was a relief to reach the steeper 100 feet curving finally into the white parabola of the col.

'Well done, old stager,' laughed Theo generously as I fetched up at his side in one last melodramatic lurch. 'You've made it all right so far.'

'Not quite so much of the old stager,' I managed to retaliate, forcing a sickly grin and bending shakily to remove my skis. 'But thanks all the same.'

The little saddle we had reached was our point of no return. Had the weather been bad, we should have been faced here with the choice between advance and retreat – quite conceivably a decision of some difficulty. As it was, the sun was shining free, there was no wind and the time was just after midday. The thought of going back never even entered our heads.

It was a delightful lunch-spot. Facing the sun, we looked out across a dazzling white corrie, a spacious amphitheatre where snow-blocks had broken from the eaves of the cornices above and lay scattered in confusion on the floor. In the opposite direction behind us an immense snow-bed, hardened to concrete by the action of the wind and frost, thrust outwards over the scoop of another, steeper corrie, Coire Cath nam Fionn. Here we looked over the edge into Glen Geusachan, 'the glen of the firs', and across to the Devil's Point, a black frown of cliffs creased and lined with snow. Higher, the background slopes climbed to a drift of mist at 4,000 feet, just touching Cairn Toul and the Angel's Peak – so called, it has been said, 'to keep the devil in his place.'

After a quarter of an hour the younger members of the party were obviously chafing to be up and doing again; the glint in their eyes betrayed what they thought of prolonged tea-breaks. So the old men had perforce to put a brave face on things and make ready for a further spell of toil.

At the cairn of Beinn Bhrotain (3,795ft), highest summit of the day.

Whoever it was that gave Monadh Mor its name – 'the big hill of the gentle slope' – can hardly have been thinking of our line of approach. The corrie on our right dropped almost vertically from under a moulding of cornices and its edge demanded considerable respect. The ascent which we actually faced was sharp enough too – 300 feet of snow so wind-hardened that it might have been beaten with hammers. The angle was never too high for our skins to grip, but it was touch and go in places and the occasional slips we did make, upsetting our rhythm annoyingly, showed the difficulty even a degree or two more would have caused.

All the way up the sun lay hot on our backs. Ski-tips thrust forward over a snow-crust that flashed like scattered diamonds. Despite thumping hearts and protesting lungs we exulted to the full in our wonderful luck with the weather.

Then quite suddenly it all changed.

The depression which, according to the forecasts, was liable to be coming in over the eastern Cairngorms, was obviously on the march. Beyond the dip of the Lairig Ghru the clouds had massed and thickened, and now there was no longer the consolation of any pools of blue. Friendliness went from the sky overhead. Glen Geusachan had taken on the black and white streakiness of a badly exposed print and it was not long before the only colour left was in the views far out to the south-west. Already the snow at our ski-tips had become grey and lacklustre.

Up on the plateau of Monadh Mor we faced a further three-quarters of a mile to the summit. But now the rise was so slight as to be barely noticeable and we pushed forward more easily, moving in silence save for the hiss of our skis. Each of us seemed withdrawn in his own thoughts. Very steadily we made ground and the few feet of height. Then, at length, centred in a sprinkling of black rocks, the diminutive, snow-plastered cairn was at our feet. The time was 1.20pm.

We stopped and someone produced a bar of chocolate. Then we bent to remove the skins from our skis, muttering as we fumbled with iced buckles and thongs.

'Well, there you are,' remarked Theo cheerfully, straightening up and waving a ski-stick toward yet another white desert that stretched out as far as ever before us. 'There's the rest of the day's work for you. It looks a bit different from the last time I was here; but then that was in June.'

Moine Mhor, 'the great moss', is one of the most interesting features of the Cairngorms. A vast upland saucer, several square miles in extent and keeping for the most part above the 3,000-foot contour, it typifies the immense scale and the loneliness, and at the same time incomparable freedom of the whole range. It is no mere desolation of peat-hags, a weariness of the flesh on a sun-baked summer's day; rather is it a place of pleasant going – fine sandy granite and springy turf, cushioned profusely with the vegetation of high-altitude alpines. The burns that have their birth on its sides flow to three great rivers, the Spey, the Feshie and the Dee, and among its knolls and hollows huge herds of deer roam. Those who have not experienced the atmosphere of Moine Mhor have not yet learnt to know the Cairngorms to the full.

Under deep snow, as we saw it, the Great Moss seemed doubly impressive. North-westwards the rim of black crags overhanging the hollow of Loch Einich and, nearer at hand, the Christmas-cake cornices above the headwaters of the River Eidart made striking landmarks. Otherwise, however, the saucer had no distinctive features: at our feet it fell away gently into a vague grey void; immeasurably far away it rose as vaguely and as gently to the ridge of Carn Ban Mor, barely distinguishable from the leaden threat of the sky. This ridge we had to reach.

The start I made could not have been described as impressive. I had dispensed with my skins, but even so the initial descent should have been simple, for the angle was favourable and the run almost entirely one straight traverse. Everything, however, seemed to have combined in a sinister conspiracy against me – the patchiness of the snow, the deceptive lighting, my growing tiredness, even one of my skis which came adrift every time I fell. Soon the others were far ahead, slowing eventually to a halt on more level ground and waiting patiently while I stumbled behind in solitary exasperation.

Yet, strangely, it was just beyond this point that I had the most enjoyable running of the whole expedition. The light had become so bad – almost the equivalent of a complete white-out – that it was impossible to judge angles or measure humps and hollows. Somehow, all the same, I managed to stay upright for what seemed a remarkably long time, keeping well up with the others and even enjoying a few turns. This was mountain travel *par excellence*, to be spun out to the last pleasant yard.

'That was grand,' I said breathlessly, as we slowed to another halt and took fresh stock of our position. 'That's the kind of running I like.'

'Well,' replied Theo, 'it was certainly a nice gentlemanly slope.' From which kindly remark I gathered that it had been only just off the level.

I had expected that the crossing of the Great Moss would mean quite simply going down one side of the saucer and up the other. But it was nothing like as straightforward as that. The middle portion is both extensive and undulating, and we even found that some of the slopes were long enough to make it worth our while putting on or removing skins. We passed the trench of the Allt Luineag, the burn which rises at over 3,500 feet on Cairn Toul and makes the main source of the Eidart. It was bridged solidly with snow. Similarly all traces of Loch nan Cnapan, the little 'lochan of the knolls', seemed to be completely hidden. In our empty grey solitude it was impossible to picture the moor hereabouts under a blue summer sky, warm and coloured, the haunt of ptarmigan and golden plover. The only living things we saw were occasional flies or spiders on the snow, blown by the wind perhaps to the middle of this vast, inhospitable desert.

It is easier now, looking back on the expedition, to appreciate how fortunate I was to have such safe companions. Any kind of mishap in the middle sections of the crossing would have been thoroughly unpleasant; indeed anything at all serious in worsening weather might have involved us in quite a struggle for survival and was simply not to be thought of. But with Theo as leader the margin of risk had been reduced to a minimum. His own skiing was faultless and he had impressed on John and Robert that any sort of dash and crash technique could have no place in cross-country work of this kind; to this the youngsters had responded admirably. His biggest concern must have been my blundering, but if it was, at least he said nothing about it. Now it was in large measure thanks to him that, as we faced the last ascent of the day, we were still in excellent order.

The climb to the Carn Ban ridge must have been all of two miles. The slope was never steep, it just went on upwards; inexorably, dispassionately upwards, as though it had had no beginning and, as surely, would have no end. There was nothing near at hand by which to measure our progress; no peat-hags, no burns, no clumps of heather. The few protruding rocks, black pinpoints of skerries in a grey-white sea, might have been ten yards away or 1000 for all we could tell; they never came any nearer. The slow passing-by of four pygmies seemed to bear no relation whatever to the remote crags of Sgor Gaoith or the cirque of Braeriach's Coire Dhondail. It was not cold. There was practically no wind. But for much of the time fine snow fell, visible against the back of the man in front as it drifted lightly down. We could only guess what it would all have been like in driving mist or blizzard. On and on we climbed, thrusting our skis mechanically forwards, endlessly up to the vague horizon of our ridge-crest.

And in the end there was nothing dramatic about our arrival. One moment we were plodding uphill, the next we had halted on a broad snowy shoulder, flat as a tennis court. There was little comment, for we were past wasting words, only muttered approval when Theo produced his flask of tea and allowed us our second drink ration of the day – a quarter of a mugful each.

The slopes which hem in the east side of Glen Feshie have always had a special attraction for skiers. Long before the crowds came teeming to Cairn Gorm, or ski-tows and *pistes* were thought of, members of the Scottish Ski Club found scope for adventurous running on the plateaux and in the sweeping corries of Carn Ban and its neighbours. In particular the corries feeding the Allt Fhearnagan, 'the alder burn', which falls to the pine woods near Achlean, gained reputations as playgrounds, their huge snow-wreaths offering wonderful scope for fast homeward runs. We had all been looking forward to this final descent from Carn Ban as the highlight of the expedition, as recompense for the hard miles that had gone before. We were confident that it would round off the day with a memorable, exhilarating climax.

It was not easy to find the best starting-point. The whole stretch of west-facing slopes had become featureless under the sombre, lowering sky. The ridges had lost distinctness, the corries between all character. To left and right stretched the same peppering of black rocks on toneless grey snow. Fingers of mist kept straying downwards, as though anxious to reach the level of Glen Feshie itself.

We skied down perhaps a couple of hundred feet to a promontory where underlying scree broke through the surface of the snow, then paused for further reconnaissance. Right at our feet stretched a magnificent unbroken ski-slope. Here was the obvious continuation. But it was set at a startlingly high angle, much higher certainly than I had expected. At mid-height it bulged out like a wind-swollen spinnaker, then slid off right-handed into a gully. The run-out below on a thin tongue of snow looked a very long way away.

For some minutes I indulged in the pleasure of picturing myself taking that slope as an expert would have done: nonchalantly pushing off; accelerating smoothly and swiftly into the fierce, breathless swoop over the bulge; here and there a check and turn; momentarily out of sight under the snow-wall, then suddenly reappearing flat out on the last narrow thread of the gully.

Then I picked up my skis and started walking down the ridge.

Some way down I stopped to watch the other three. Even at a distance it was obvious that they were enjoying themselves immensely. For the steeper sections they kept close formation, zig-zagging methodically and turning with studied care. But once the angles began to ease, the discipline that had served so well throughout the day went to the winds and they scattered to choose their own individual lines down the final few hundred feet. I was happy to be a spectator this time, no longer a drag on the party. It all looked so simple and yet such tremendous fun. Certainly this last downhill running was everything that might have been desired. There could have been no more satisfying climax to the journey.

We joined up again on the heather, not far now from Achlean. Outside the farmhouse the car was parked; apparently everything had gone well with Thelma on her long drive round over Drumochter. We had been spotted high on Carn Ban and now we were welcomed at the farm to the luxury of deep armchairs and a blazing fire. Mrs Clark, the farmer's wife, was losing no time in busying herself with one of the biggest teapots I have ever seen.

When eventually, in drowsy contentment, we continued on our way down the glen, the light was failing rapidly. Automatically we looked back towards the plateau of Carn Ban. Its edge was indistinguishable in the grey depths of the clouds. There was still little or no wind, but the mist-fringe was trailing lower across the vague face of the snow. Soon it would be quite dark.

Up there the solitude was complete.

Chapter Fifteen

TWO OLDIES AND THE GAICK – 1995

ROUGHLY parallel to the road over Drumochter, the Gaick pass climbs and drops
for 21 miles through a wilderness of desolate, steeply-angled hills. From Dalnacardoch, five miles south of Dalnaspidal on the A9, it cuts through to Tromie
Bridge, near Kingussie, on Speyside.

According to what we read, a crossing on bikes would be 'a real challenge; an excellent
introduction to hill pass cycling.' Certainly it seemed to have all the ingredients of a day to
remember for my wife and myself – just the job for starting us off on a suitable new diet of
old folk adventuring.

According to another description, 'The Gaick has the most evil reputation of any place
in the Highlands.' One reason for this notoriety, we learned, is that outsize avalanches have
a way of raking the path lethally in winter and spring. The name Gaick is from the Gaelic
gag, meaning a 'cleft', and this seemingly described perfectly the narrow middle section
imprisoned by bare, plunging hillsides. Huge snow-slides, resulting in not a few fatalities,
had made it a place to be scrupulously avoided at the wrong time of the year.

Contributing also to the evil reputation of 'dark Gaick of the crooked ravines' was the
legacy left by the Black Officer of Ballachroan, Captain John MacPherson. His recruiting
methods for the Army of his day were so wickedly devious and so cruelly unscrupulous
that they even came to be suspected of having more than a touch of the occult. Perhaps it
was only justice that the Captain should have perished along with four companions in a
Gaick bothy overwhelmed by a terrible avalanche at New Year 1800.

It was, of course, precisely when the avalanches would be avalanching that Mais and I
first had the notion to go. We could only wait impatiently as spring slipped past, looking
forward to dates suiting the friends we had hoped might go with us. Then summer came,
in 1995 the hottest and longest of heatwaves within most living memories – ideal for river-
crossings, far too oppressive for hard work. There was nothing to do but study the maps,
read the descriptions, measure and remeasure the miles. We even made a few feeble
attempts to get into training. And so in the autumn – despite a deal of kindly head-shaking
– we decided to go it alone.

That is – if we could meet last-minute objections in the ranks by borrowing a mobile
phone…

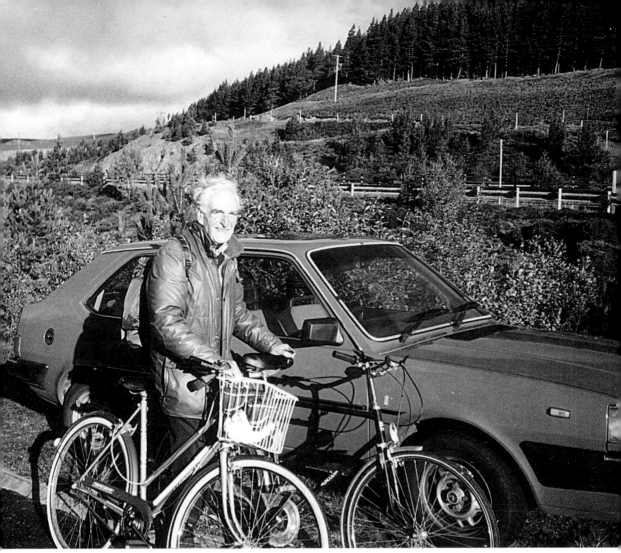

Autumn journey. Ready to start off for the crossing of the Gaick.

As back-up team our good friends and neighbours Stan and Margaret Stirton had nobly agreed to meet us at journey's end, uplift us and bear us safely home, hopefully in triumph. And they had a mobile phone which they would kindly lend us. So Stan and I took it out and tested for signals in several possibly typical places around Aberfeldy. Results were satisfactory. Mutiny was averted. Final arrangements were agreed.

The Big Day itself was 28 September, our arrival time at Dalnacardoch shortly before nine o'clock. As we fumbled to unload the cycles (our everyday machines, not the awe-inspiring, multi-geared mountain bikes we had been kindly offered) the wind tugged at us. It was cold. In the distance the higher tops were peppered white with new snow. It was amusing to reflect how it had been while we were waiting for the previous winter's snows to melt that we had first been chafing to get going. Things had come very nearly full circle.

A Land-Rover drew up beside us. 'Where were you thinking of making for?' The young keeper eyed us and our bikes keenly.

'Hopefully over the Gaick,' we replied, rather obviously.

'Well, there's a stalk on today,' he commented. 'The deer are down low just now.' We accepted the point. 'It's a right of way, though,' we countered.

'Yes, but there's a hellish wind up along the loch today'. Our grey-white locks blowing in the breeze were doubtless presenting a question mark. 'Well anyway, at least see and keep to the path, please.'

He waved us on our way, doubtless thinking already of the rescue helicopter that would be on standby at Kinloss.

It was good to get going, satisfying to face the first of the day's hazards – dodging the traffic as we wheeled our bikes across the A9 to the stony start of the track. At once we had to climb, through an old wood that crowded in on us. Quickly the traffic noises were deadened, already a thousand miles away.

'A bit like the Strohsack,' remarked Mais, thinking back to that honeymoon day lang syne, when we had followed the pine-scented path up a fine hill in Austria. Doubtless in those days our speed uphill was more impressive. But what matter? We were making light enough of the initial 300 feet – and enjoying it too. We passed, a little surprisingly, three or four forestry men busy at work. Then, shortly after, we were quit of the trees, on our own, with moorland and the open road ahead.

For four-and-a-half miles our route now kept close to the Edendon Water, a lively burn fed initially by sources high on the Munros north-east of Drumochter and flowing eventually into the Garry at Dalnacardoch. Well above its trench to begin with, we idled gradually down to its level and a bridge to its west bank, half way to Sronphadruig Lodge.

One of my concerns beforehand had been that the surface of our Land-Rover track might consist in part of stones so large and flinty-edged that they could buckle the wheels of our cycles. This was in fact a worry for much of the day, but it was only really justified on short, steep descents which were particularly brutal. And at these we were mindful to dismount and walk.

We found the level stretch of track beyond the bridge one of the most enjoyable of the day. The Edendon had a diamond sparkle and, although far from full, a welcoming song to match. The sun was warm on our backs, and the wind, which admittedly faced us with an unwelcome touch of north in it, gusted only occasionally with any strength. Even the concreted ford which we knew to expect half a mile short of the Lodge had only inches of water to lap over our boots. We wondered, in fact, when all the trials and tribulations would be confronting us.

We need not have worried; they were to be coming soon enough.

Nearing the Lodge we were confronted by a Land-Rover and a second young keeper. No doubt his eye had been upon us and our bikes for some time. Predictably the conversation mixture was much as before. Were we aware that stalking was in progress? Where were we bound for? Would we be sure and keep to the path? Having reassured him on all counts, we proceeded on our harmless way.

TWO OLDIES AND THE GAICK – 1995

Untenanted and shuttered, Sronphadruig Lodge stood aloof a short distance from the track. In its scattering of trees it looked huge and dark and not a little forbidding. Yet for us it was in reality an encouraging landmark. We had put six miles satisfactorily behind us and so, with things going so well, there was no need to think of the Lodge as a sensible turning-point before we became caught up in the more serious work of the day. We sat down on a grandstand of stones and took optimistic stock over an egg sandwich.

There was more than a touch of deception to the next small section of our route. The track swung in a wide leftward arc alongside the Edendon, then straightened alluringly once more. And there lay the catch. Easily missed on the far bank of the burn, an ancient wooden sign, tilted drunkenly and marked almost illegibly 'Gaick', fingerpointed the true route up an unpleasantly steep bank. A ragged path, of which not even the hardiest of blackfaces would have approved, led up this face in steps of rock and slippery peat. To have climbed this unencumbered would have been a simple if perhaps messy matter; with the two bicycles it was a less joyous task. Take-off was from a swirl of water in the burn itself and toeholds in the peat higher up were not particularly reassuring.

We did make a much-needed pause half way up and we were amused to see, as we looked back to Sronphadruig, that our friend in the Land-Rover had moved to a more advantageous position for keeping tab on our movements. He would have had the glass on us no doubt and we wondered if maybe he had been taking malicious delight in noting that we were quite literally sticking to the path. Of the deer-stalking activities we had heard mentioned there was neither sound nor sight.

The sheep-path was our highway for the next one-and-a-half miles, a muddy switchback little more than a foot or two wide. Above and beyond the initial bank we were able to look along the length of Loch an Duin, previously not visible to us down at the level of the Edendon. The loch lies in a deep hollow between twin Corbetts, An Dun (2,713ft) and Maol Creag an Loch (2,874ft), aptly described in the Scottish Mountaineering Club guide as 'walled about by some of the steepest and most unrelenting hill slopes in Scotland.' So fiercely steep indeed are these slopes that it is easily seen how avalanche-prone they must be in winter and spring, and thus how they have come by their evil reputation.

As we followed our wispy gallery scarring the flank of An Dun, we could not help recalling the warning we had been given of exposure high above the loch. We kept expecting some hazard at every fresh bend, but there was nothing untoward; even with the bikes to bump along with us, we never felt close to a slither into the loch. And of the stalker's 'hellish' wind that was to harry us so mercilessly there was scarcely a whisper; all I remember, indeed, is the music of the ripples lapping the southern shore, that typically nostalgic tune of countless Highland lochans.

At the further, northern end the slope of An Dun finally relented and merged in an anti-climax of flat stony beach. A section of the route which had seemed likely to be troublesome was now safely behind us.

The Loch an Duin test had indeed been successfully passed, but another and tougher loomed large almost at once: the outflow from the loch, the Allt Loch an Duin, had somehow to be crossed. And it had a not very welcoming look.

With commendable, if unwonted, foresight we had brought pairs of ancient gym-shoes with us to put on in order to keep boots and socks from being soaked during river-crossings. We changed therefore and advanced, bicycles in hand, to the fray.

Unfortunately we chose a very poor crossing-place. Certainly the first few ankle-deep yards were almost enjoyable. But then trouble started: the depth deepened, the current quickened, the stones started slithering – and the bicycles took over. Back wheels jammed between boulders, saddles dug us in the ribs, handlebars slewed round 180 degrees in the hostile swirl. At which point all we felt strong enough to do was give in and sit down. Yet the far bank still remained – a few awkward feet of peaty verticality. And so, with a couple of heaves inspired by desperation, we finally landed, spent but exultant, on a haven of flat turf.

'All I can say,' I muttered once I had some of my breath back, 'is, thank goodness it was the driest summer spell in living memory.'

'And all I can say,' replied Mais, 'is, I hate river-crossings.'

'Well, anyway,' I went on, 'if I remember aright, the next one should be a bit easier. I think the book says it is more of a nuisance than a difficulty.'

'*Another* crossing?' questioned my wife, looking kind of different. 'We've crossed two rivers and a ford already. And – forgive me if I'm wrong – but you did say… and by the way, while you're about it, do you mind telling me, please, why I couldn't have married someone who was a mere Scrabble maniac, or maybe just an ordinary country dance enthusiast?'

'Yes, of course,' I ventured meekly. 'And what do you think the weather's going to do? I wonder if it's a bit like a storm is brewing up?'

Thankfully we were now at the start of another Land-Rover track. Back once more on our bikes, we pedalled a further pleasurable mile or so. It was just coming on for two o'clock. Another sitting of lunch seemed called for.

We chose a pleasant, sheltered spot beside a protective boulder and hoped that our ice-chilled feet would begin to thaw out. Opposite us, beyond the Allt Loch an Duin, was a fine corrie cupped in a cirque of tawny hills; ahead, we had a splendid view along Loch Bhrodainn, next loch of the day. It was good to sit and relax.

It was here that we decided to try out the mobile phone – a place not too shut in, yet not too open either; a fair choice, we thought. I pulled out the precious instrument from the cocooned depths of my rucksack and went through the button-pressing ritual. There was not the faintest suggestion of a signal. (Nor indeed was there any when we tried again once or twice later in the afternoon).

Half way over the Gaick pass. Maisie and bicycle above Loch an Duin.

'Just as well,' commented Mais significantly, 'that we didn't have a preview of this last night. And,' she continued even more significantly, 'it certainly makes me wonder what we'd have done if anything had happened to one or other of us hereabouts? I wouldn't have known whether to try going back or carrying on, and a night alone with the Black Officer etc to haunt me wouldn't be all that much fun. In fact, are we really all that sensible being here at all?'

To which, of course, there was no answer.

Leaving such defeatist talk behind, we pedalled on blithely towards Loch Bhrodainn. The track was kindly, with relatively few troublesome bumps, so we made excellent time for another mile. Alongside the loch, too, we were further cheered by the sight of Gaick Lodge itself. But always at the back of our minds was the thought of that next river.

A mile short of the Lodge we paused. Down on our left, at the foot of a steep, rough slope, was our old friend, the Allt Loch an Duin, but looking strangely different – black, sluggish, obviously very deep. At that particular moment it suggested nothing so much as one of the less attractive reaches of the Liverpool-Manchester ship canal.

'So,' muttered my companion at length, with a smile of questionable sweetness, 'is this it? Because if it is, I'm away home.'

'Hang on a minute,' I ventured, not wishing to push things too far by recalling the way we had come. 'I'm sure things will take on a new look once we're round the next bend or two.' We continued in silence, maybe a fraction stony.

Then, all of a sudden, I remembered. The crossing we had to tackle was over a sizeable burn, but coming in from a glen on our right, not over the Allt Loch an Duin at all. In a moment everything was different. Hope revived. Optimism was back. Our pedals started turning again to an altogether cheerier tune.

We followed the fringe of an old grey wood, swung out and down round a bend, and there ahead was the crossing – wide indeed, but nowhere deep, nowhere fierce-flowing, leading to a flat, easy-angled exit. We were quickly across, bicycles and all, laughing now that our fears had been groundless. Then we sat down, tried to find some traces of life in our feet, and put on dry boots and socks.

Unfortunately our new glow of comfort was not long-lived. A heavy shower which had been drifting in an ominous curtain across the face of Sgor Dearg, to the west, overtook us shortly after our restart. We stopped, donned waterproof clothing, then pedalled on past the gate of Gaick Lodge. A wisp of smoke from one of the chimneys tantalisingly suggested a warm fireside chair and a cup or two of tea.

Strangely enough, Loch an t-Seilich, 'loch of the willow', the largest of the day's three lochs, was the one which made the least impression. Perhaps we were tiring a little, or perhaps we were concentrating less because the hardest of our problems were past, but certainly I recollect few outstanding details. The rain squall had blown over and the track, although climbing towards the far end of the loch, was not so steep as to be toilsome; it was partially wooded, too, so that there was little sense of height such as there had been above Loch an Duin.

Impatience was now giving new zest to our pedalling – half a mile on, the Glen Tromie hydro-electric dam would see the start of a tarmac road. It seemed almost outrageously slow in appearing.

There could have been no more satisfying climax to the day than the descent of Glen Tromie from the dam to Tromie Bridge: almost nine miles of traffic-free road, all downhill or amiably level, with a light breeze for occasional help – surely any cyclist's dream. It was particularly good as an end to the crossing – no thoughts now of the rough miles, of mobile phones, of ice-cold rivers, only the wind singing in our ears as we exulted in by far the most amazing freewheel either of us had ever experienced.

We stopped twice. Once for a brief roadside snack, as a skein of some twenty geese passed overhead, wrangling, with weariness maybe near the end of a much more taxing journey than ours. They were the only birds we had seen all day except for a pair of teal, exploding suddenly from an edge of marshland near Gaick Lodge.

We paused too at the boundary of the Gaick estate, where a gate barred the way at a bridge over a deep-cut defile and burn. The gate sported a formidable array of chains and padlocks, making it look as though a Herculean lift of our steeds would be

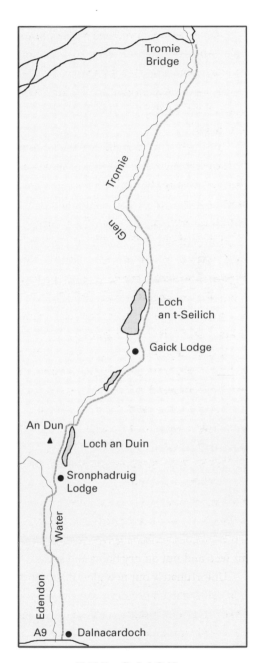

THE GAICK

Miles

0 1 2 3 4 5

necessary. However, none of the padlocks was actually secured, so that our passage to freedom was simple.

At 17.07 hours precisely the two oldies dismounted at Tromie Bridge. The crossing had taken exactly 7 hours and 47 minutes. For mountain bikes and youngsters our guide book had suggested five hours plus halts.

The day's pleasures were not quite at an end. As arranged, our unfailingly kind support team duly arrived to collect us. We were surprised nevertheless that we were, briefly, first at Tromie Bridge. Knowing Stan and Margaret, we had expected them to be waiting for us, not at all probably the other way round. We soon learned why. Leaving Aberfeldy in excellent time, they had come fully half way, then in a sudden less than happy moment realised that they had forgotten to bring the roof-rack fitment for the bicycles. Nobly they had turned back and, doubtless at breakneck speed, remedied the omission. Now they were as generous in their welcome as we were grateful to them. Without delay they had us and the bikes aboard the car; then we headed back south, appetites running riot as we contemplated a celebration bar meal half way down the road home to Aberfeldy.

Chapter Sixteen

CORRIEYAIRACK – 1996

FOR years the logistics of doing the Corrieyairack with our bicycles had been a maddening puzzle for Mais and me. Like the problem of getting the fox and goose single-handed across the river, it seemed to have a non-existent answer. Even when, for a while, we had a caravan ideally in situ at Fort Augustus, we failed to come up with any simple solution. It was only when our good friends and collaborators on the Gaick, Stan and Margaret Stirton, kindly agreed to co-operate once again, that the twin worries of transport and safety back-up began to fade. At last fancy looked like becoming fact.

It is often said that General Wade's masterpiece was the elegant bridge over the River Tay at Aberfeldy. Surely, however, an equal triumph – certainly in road engineering – was his high-level route from Upper Speyside over the Corrieyairack pass to Fort Augustus. For us, with its challenging miles and unique niche in Scottish history, the crossing had an appeal which quite simply was not to be resisted.

For long before 1731, when Wade's road was built, the Corrieyairack had been well known and well used, most notably by the drovers and their black cattle converging from north and west to head over the pass to the great market trysts of the Lowlands. Back in February 1645, Montrose 'the great marquis' had led his army over the hills from the Great Glen and down Glen Roy to make their historic surprise attack on Inverlochy. A century later, in August 1745, Prince Charles Edward, in buoyant mood in the early days of his campaign, was to make further history when he crossed southwards over the pass with his Highlanders. Far differently the following year he was to make the crossing again during his tragic flight in the heather.

For Mais and me the chief hazard seemed to be the state of the track itself. We had heard ominous reports that excessive use by four-wheel-drive vehicles had rendered the surface miserably unpleasant. For mountain bikers things might just be tolerable; for oldies on 'ordinary' machines things could be very different. However, we were still more than a little pleased with ourselves after the previous year's success on the Gaick and were looking for a fresh challenge, even if we were that year older – both of us. If Montrose and his men could manage the crossing in February snow and reputedly on empty stomachs, could there be any excuses for well-fed summer shirking on our part?

Melgarve. Meall garbh, 'rough lump of a hill.' An apt description for our starting-point. Especially on a dull July morning with a drift of mist on the hills. It was cold, too, not helpful for morale. However, Stan and Margaret soon joined us and a note of optimism was restored. The plan was for them to take over our car and drive in it the 62 miles round to Fort Augustus, then walk north-south over the pass. Thus, all going well, we should meet up some distance beyond the highest point as we made our way downhill – a useful provision, we had decided, for that safety factor which we like to have nowadays in our not-so-youthful state. We exchanged cheery goodbyes. The time was almost 10.30. It was to be some five hours before we were greeting them again on the far side of the pass.

The track went uphill. Straight uphill – typically Wade. In parts as rough as a Munro scree-run. The beginning of a pattern for the day. Mais tried a defiant 20 yards on her bike, then had to dismount smartly. My own attempt to do better ended equally abruptly and less gracefully in a sideways slither into the ditch. Soon, however, we were 'peching' on foot upwards, always expecting better things. Unfortunately the better things remained conspicuous by their absence.

We had our first breather after a quarter of a mile, when three mountain bikers caught up with us and paused briefly for a chat. We had been highly impressed by the way they made progress appear to be almost childishly easy – big stones, little stones, round stones, square stones, all seemed to be treated with equal nonchalance – their determination making it look as if it would be against the rules to dismount. It was clear from what they said that they had a high performance rating; indeed we began to feel we really ought to commiserate with them because the Corrieyairack was too simple. We made one final effort to retrieve the situation.

'How about the Gaick?' we queried. 'Have you thought of that?'

'Yes, well actually we have. We're doing it tomorrow.' At which point conversation flagged and we waved them off again on their way. In no time at all, it seemed, they were barely distinguishable against the final grey of the long initial straight.

Later in the day and well down the far side of the pass, the three were to meet Stan and Margaret. Remarkably, the latter told us that our mountain bikers had reported having had to cope with six punctures.

We ourselves were amazed, not very much further on, to see on looking back two or three cars making heavy weather of a particularly nasty section of track. At first we decided they were stuck and in dire trouble. Eventually, however, they got going again and quickened their tortoise-creep sufficiently to catch us up. They proved to be the first of a 24-strong Scottish Sports Tours party, consisting of Belgian, French and Dutch four-wheel-drive vehicles bound for the summit of the pass and back. They were a cheery crowd and eyed us curiously, obviously certain that the two old dears were about to collapse in a heap. 'Are you sure you're OK?' asked one driver solicitously. And another, equally concerned, 'How about a bottle of Belgian beer?' The only trouble was that for each car that passed we had to move off the track and as this whole procedure had to be gone through again as we met them later on their return journey, we could only wonder if pushing our bikes might well have been less frustrating on Sauchiehall Street than on the lonely Corrieyairack.

The track swung right-handed – still straight, still mainly uphill – above the trench of the Allt Yairack and into the wide sweep of Corrie Yairack itself. By now the cars were making slightly better time and soon we could see the leaders well ahead, creeping upwards like beetles on Wade's famous traverses, or zigzags, scarring the steep far wall of the corrie.

All this while we had been so immersed in our tussle with the track, riding and walking alternately, that we had taken little notice of the weather. Not indeed that it would have given much cause for rejoicing – dull cloud cover with an occasional hint of drizzle had matched the bleakness of the moors. However, to give us some much needed encouragement, we were welcomed at the foot of the traverses by a generous sun-blink. It seemed a good omen.

We toiled up a zig and a zag and sat down on a couple of boulders. 'Well anyway,' I remarked, 'that's two we've done.'

'How do you mean – two?' The question was not altogether unexpected. 'How many more are there? I don't seem to remember your telling me.'

'Only another eleven,' I ventured. 'That's according to the book. But of course some of these books can be hopelessly inaccurate.' I just hoped that the sun would continue its encouraging blink.

Breath more or less back, we resumed our push up the slope. In fact it went remarkably easily. We were just starting along the thirteenth traverse when we were met by all the 24 cars coming down. The drivers seemed cheery and carefree as ever, though clearly with a wary eye on the slope. However much we might have preferred having the corrie to ourselves, we could hardly help admiring the intrepid driving that was needed. Indeed, looking back down the wall it was easier now to understand the wildly imaginative comments of some of the early travellers as they faced the route in some rickety coach or on the back of a restive horse.

One traveller who risked a north-south crossing by carriage found the whole road 'inexpressibly arduous' and told of 'pursuing narrow ridges of rock frightfully impending over tremendous precipices.' In 1798 another traveller, who chose horseback, reported 'wild desolation beyond anything he could describe and the whole of the road rough, dangerous and dreadful, even for a horse.' He had wretched weather, for at the top of the zigzags he thought he and the horse 'would be carried away, he knew not whither, so strong was the blast, so hard the rain, and so very thick the mist.' By comparison our fair-weather bicycle push-over certainly seemed remarkably tame. Nevertheless, as we watched our continental visitors disappearing down the far-from-kindly wall behind us, we could not help wondering if some future versions might not be going to match those tales of the past for hair-raising exaggeration.

I had fondly imagined that once we were clear of the zigzags our upward toiling would be over. I was too optimistic; the top of the pass was still quite some distance higher. Originally there had been a further five traverses here (later straightened) and we could well have done with their help. As it was, we found the plod particularly hard, a dunt to morale that was more than a little tiresome.

Apart from a certain amount of hydro-electric ironmongery, the pass itself had little of interest to offer. Even the far views coloured in so attractively in other descriptions – from the Aonachs and Ben Nevis to Kintail, Glen Affric and more besides – were mostly curtained by low cloud. We contented ourselves with thoughts of hard work accomplished and a nice easy future, downhill all the way. We recalled that happy ending to the Gaick, those glorious freewheel miles all the way down Glen Tromie.

For a short distance all seemed plain sailing – a level stretch even pleasantly rideable. This, we decided, was more like it; if the remaining eight miles were to be all like this, we'd be at journey's end in no time. But it was not to be. No way were our troubles over. The track took a slanting line, gradually dropping into the grassy bowl of Coire Uchdachan. Downhill admittedly. But the rideable sections had again become very few, very far between. We were back to the old familiar jagged, jarring, rough, rocky, painful patches over which we had to trudge. It was more than time for lunch.

We escaped from the chill of the breeze behind a large boulder and enjoyed our snack to the full. We looked west to the unmistakable near-Munro cone of Ben Tee, beside it the seven-mile silver of Loch Garry. More often, however, our gaze strayed down the next quarter-mile of track to where it disappeared round a corner above the Allt Coire Uchdachan, reckoning it was about then that Stan and Margaret should be appearing.

Time, all the same, was catching up on us, so as there was no sign of them, we moved on. In fact, the pleasure of the meeting was not long deferred. Our friends were in excellent form, going strong and with no misadventures to report. They even did their best to highlight the better stretches of the track which lay ahead of us – sadly all too brief a catalogue. For our part, we tried equally hard to underplay the length of the miles in front of them. Their north-south walk, started at an altitude 1,100 feet lower than at Melgarve, was a tougher proposition than ours. Consequently we had been concerned lest they might feel they had drawn a particularly short straw. How wrong we were! All went well with the remainder of their crossing and they assured us afterwards that they had had no such feelings, only real elation to have 'done the Corrieyairack.'

Our next excuse for lying flat and relaxing was two miles further on, at Snugburgh. Here the track, rough as a lava-field, zigzags abruptly down to a Bailey bridge crossing another burn, the Allt Lagan a' Bhainne. Nearby, an expanse of turf, attractively green and level, has the look of an ideal campsite and was in fact where Wade and his 500 'highwaymen' celebrated the completion of the road on 30 October 1731 with six whole oxen, roasted on six fires, and their own brewed beer – hence the apt nickname, Snugburgh. Four o'clock and now pleasantly sunny – we were greatly tempted to linger, even having

Facing a tiresome rise before the final descent of the Corrieyairack.

been welcomed by a grey wagtail and a willow warbler, surprised into song, the only signs of bird life all day, apart from an occasional meadow pipit.

Unfortunately it was another uphill grind out of our sanctuary and we felt suitably aggrieved. It was the first of not a few climbs we were to be facing before journey's end, but the surroundings were to be enjoyed – in place of bleak hill-slopes, greenery of bracken and birches hiding the deep-set gorge of the Tarff. We met a trio of cyclists, one a girl, on 'ordinary' machines. Bound for Newtonmore over the pass, they told us. We wondered how they would fare. The day was not exactly young.

The three miles which we still had to cover might perhaps have been kindly described as a memorable mixture. Unexpectedly we had the encouragement of a fine bird's eye glimpse of Fort Augustus, only to have it snatched from our hungry gaze as the track wandered away unhelpfully westwards. For a while the actual surface continued to be thoroughly tiresome, so tiresome in fact that I resorted to timing the stretches that we found rideable. The record – equalled twice – was exactly 65 seconds; over and over again we had to dismount after only 15 or 20 in the saddle. Then briefly, after another dip and climb, matters improved and we had the only joyful freewheeling stretch of the day.

We dropped more slowly past Culachy House and its reed-edged duck pond and then there remained only the final quarter-mile. It looked impossible – impossible to ride and, with bikes, almost impossible to stagger over. It resembled nothing so much as a drystane dyke lying on its side. Alongside its tortured twists there was not even a thread of a path that a reasonably nimble sheep might have fancied. At the end of our long day it was hardly the kind of climax we might have wished for. In the event it took us all our time to hump and bump the bikes to the gate that marked the end of the way. There, prominently displayed, a notice informed us that, as the Corrieyairack is now classified as an ancient monument, anyone found damaging it in any way would be answerable to the Secretary of State.

The time was exactly seven o'clock; we had been hard at it for eight-and-a-half hours. And interestingly enough, while my estimate for the climb to the top of the pass had been remarkably exact, that for the descent had been 'out' by no less than three full hours: the reason, our ups and downs of mounting and dismounting for so much of the way down. The lesson had clearly been that non-mountain bikes are much better left tucked up at home.

The fleshpots of Fort Augustus were unmixed pleasure. Not simply because of the old adage that banging the head against a wall is enjoyable for the wonderful feeling of relief when it is all over. Maybe, to be honest, there *was* something of that – especially for two who, just maybe, were feeling their years. But the real satisfaction came from knowing that General Wade's long-standing challenge had been met at last; that there would always be a whole world of interest to remember, quite apart from one of hard flints and potholed puddles. We have no plans for doing the traverse again.

Journey's end. The final stretch of the Corrieyairack track.

Chapter Seventeen

THE STORY OF A BOOK

FOR Maisie MacKintosh Saturday 23 June 1962 was a date that would never be forgotten. Not indeed that in advance the weekend ahead had looked to be anything but straightforward. Along with friends from Aberdeen, John and Sandra Morgan, Maisie was due to make up a foursome on her fiancé Jock Pirrit's yacht *Suva*, the intention being to enjoy some ordinary Clyde cruising round about the Cumbraes.

On the following Monday evening Maisie was to be attending as guest at a dinner party celebrating the end of session at Queen's College in Glasgow where she was a lecturer in nutrition and dietetics – an annual student event to which class teachers were customarily invited.

All perfectly simple – until a complication arose.

One of Maisie's class, a popular Indian girl, was summoned home early because of some family trouble. Hurriedly, on her account, the dinner date was brought forward from the Monday to the Saturday evening.

And so for Maisie the question arose – attend the dinner party or opt for the sailing? Duty won. She joined her students.

During that Saturday evening Maisie kept wondering how the three on *Suva* were faring. Sandra had been especially glad that she was to have Maisie with her on the yacht. She was a novice and not a little scared. It would have been good to have had her company.

That night a ferocious freak storm hit Scotland's west coast. *Suva* was torn from her mooring off Millport, her anchor chain severed under the strain. Somewhere in mid-channel in the blackness and the buffeting and the chaos she broke up and foundered. All three on board, John, Sandra and Jock, were lost.

Next day, Sunday, Maisie saw and heard the news on television. The bodies had been washed ashore near Wemyss Bay. She was devastated.

* * * * *

Turn elsewhere now, briefly, for the further telling of this story, to a different part of Glasgow but that same summer of 1962. As related in an earlier chapter, it was a time that dragged impossibly slowly past for the children and me. Or perhaps, thinking back on it now, was it not all in fact brutally brief? It was the ending of the five-year spell of illness suffered by my wife Helen; finally, as the summer faded, the parting of the last September evening.

As a family we tried as best we could to achieve the impossible – to find consolation,

Helen and John and their mother, Wengen 1959.

consolation for each of us individually and for us all. We had nonetheless to learn the bitterness of having to tread the path of desolation. For myself I realise now only too well how sadly I failed with my daughter Helen and son John – especially the latter who was only nine at the time. Not indeed that we lacked for help. Many, very many friends were more than kind and thoughtful – and we got by.

But kindness, however warm and loving and sincere, is simply not enough. There has to be more, very much more.

My Christian faith has ever tended now and again to need a deal of polishing. Yet always, thankfully, it has been there for the grasping. And so, even in the long hours of tunnel dark, I found light shining out. Every night indeed, when morale had its way of plumbing bleak depths, before turning to sleep, I found unfailing comfort in my readings. Especially to finish, it had to be the last words of Matthew's gospel: 'Lo, I am with you alway, even unto the end of the world.'

I discovered too the words of Katharina von Schlegel's great hymn *Be still, my soul*, set so movingly to the theme music of Sibelius' *Finlandia*. Read and re-read over and over, it had words of comfort impossible not to contemplate and clutch and take to heart.

And that, though I didn't know it, was the starting point of an entirely new path.

Now and again, very occasionally over the years as the notion took me, I had been in the habit of noting brief quotes of special appeal – a verse maybe or some unique saying that seemed a nugget worth the treasuring. It was the sort of apparently useless collection of vagrant scraps and jottings so many people fancy storing, then leave more than half forgotten in the corner of some dusty drawer.

Happening one day for no apparent reason to look at the tattered old notebook I used, my attention was caught by one or two quotes which seemed particularly applicable to our time of family sadness; only one or two and I cannot remember which, yet precisely so striking that they couldn't be ignored and passed by.

Why not, I wondered, make a proper collection? Not just haphazard but put together with set purpose. A small book, maybe, but primarily of hope and help in a Christian context. At least, however modest, it would be worth a try. And so, as ideas came tumbling in, a start was made. Surprisingly the collection began to grow. It was to be 26 years before it was completed.

Little did I suspect in those early days that a very special fillip to the planning, with immense encouragement to match, was not far round the corner. In the late summer of 1965 I met Maisie for the first time.

After the tragic loss of her friends on board *Suva*, it had been hard beyond words for Maisie. In Glasgow the college year was officially at an end, but she still had to teach a week's summer course, an almost impossibly trying task to have to fight through. It was, in fact, no more than a tense putting in of time until the next Sunday evening, when she had asked to go with her friend and colleague, Marion, to the service at the city centre church, St George's Tron. (And Marion, faithful friend as she was, stayed behind for that express purpose instead of going home to Skye.)

Regularly crowded to the doors on Sunday evenings, 'the Tron' at that time had as minister the late Rev Tom Allan. And Mr Allan was very special. Maisie had the sure and certain conviction that his words could bring her the message she yearned for: a message of understanding and comfort, even a glimmer of hope reborn. And in the event there was indeed that overwhelming flood of assurance and peace. Yet also, immeasurably more than that, Maisie knew a profound conversion experience. All down the years things were never to be the same again.

In the summer break that followed there was further blessing for her, as she was able to accept the invitation of good friends to get away with them for a spell to the consoling balm of Iona. Those three weeks of peace and healing have remained a very special memory. Almost every summer since as the years have passed there has been a return to the island, a recapturing of the blessing that once meant so much.

Further happiness too, of a different, very special kind, was to follow for Mais and me after that meeting which we had in the summer of 1965: on the ensuing first of April we were married in a small church not far from Glasgow – a quiet wedding on an unforgettably beautiful spring day.

By that time my collection of quotations had straggled forward well beyond its first unimpressive disarray. Swift progress all the same was not exactly its hallmark. What was needed for me to get a move on was a lively second opinion. Mais provided exactly that with an accompanying vital spark of enthusiasm. With her initiative more nuggets were discovered, more striking groupings chosen. Morale took a real turn for the better.

In due course also, some two decades later, we were to be benefiting from the literary wisdom of our son Kenneth, along with something of his own poetry.

One joint idea which Mais and I put successfully into practice was to show the collection to the late Jack Knox, at that time managing director of John Smith & Son, the well-known Glasgow booksellers. I had worked in Smith's for a short time after the war and knew Jack well. Mais too knew him, although in a different way. Her fiancé Jock Pirrit, who lost his life in the *Suva* tragedy, had travelled widely as an explorer, and a book which he had written, *Across West Antarctica*, was being prepared for posthumous publication by John Smith's. Mais had come to know Jack Knox in the course of this work as she provided personal details and reminiscences of Jock's life and achievements. We went therefore to see Jack, looking for his advice and, to be strictly honest, maybe his commendation also. He did indeed give ready approval of the book idea itself and kindly offered to approach a few possible publishers. Not surprisingly he had no success. For a well-known politician, a celebrated general or a TV personality the door can be wide-open; for a mere struggling mortal it is rarely even ajar. Anthologies, we were told, are simply not wanted by publishers; quite apart from any other reason, permissions for copyright material can cost a prohibitive amount of time and money.

Despite such setbacks the book took shape, albeit very gradually and with much stumbling. Overall the central theme was to be a climb from the depths, a progression from darkness to light. Each week was given a separate heading – Desolation, The Troubles of Others, Hope in Dark Days, Choice, Commitment, Trust and so on. In theory each of these was also to be a progression in itself, but this turned out to be too difficult to achieve; often pieces for six days would almost select themselves, only to have the seventh proving elusive.

When two or three more approaches to publishers – in the States as well as in the UK – had failed dismally, our hopes dropped to new depths. We had come to what looked ominously like the end of the road. The manuscript was consigned to a suitably deep cupboard, there to collect over the months a fresh coating of dust.

Then, strangely enough through the head of a publishing house, a glimmer of fresh hope shone through. During the war I had known slightly the Rev John Birkbeck MC, who had been a chaplain with the Army Commandos and associated notably with the successful 'heavy water' raid in Norway. Sadly John died in 1989, but 20 years previously he had left the parish ministry to become director of the Drummond Press in Stirling. It was at that time, in 1970, that I thought of asking him to evaluate the anthology, then still in its rather topsy-turvy state.

He could not possibly have been more helpful. Kindness itself with his comments, he was so enthusiastic that he even went so far as to say, 'This simply must be published.' Unfortunately, for financial reasons, his own firm was not in a position to undertake the actual work. But the timing of his encouragement was exactly right. The uplift to morale came just when it was most needed. All of a sudden the pieces began to come together, to slot quite remarkably into place.

We had, for example, been giving a deal of thought to the choice of a title. Early on, bogged down in a stodge of banality, we could not get beyond *A Memorial Christian Anthology*. Then one night Mais had a dream. She was in a well-known bookshop in Fort William putting in time with a haphazard browse. Just then a customer came into the shop. Approaching the assistant he asked: 'Have you got a copy of *An Anthology of Hope?*' We had been given our title!

So far as obtaining the many necessary copyright permissions was concerned, we knew to expect a long hard slog. Just how long and gruelling it was to be we could not have guessed. It was in fact to cost me a full year of toil and an outlay of between £800 and £900, the latter fortunately covered by a very generous Drummond Trust grant.

Looking back on all that work now, it is amusing to recall some of the many odd twists and quirks. Individual writers, for example, seemed to suffer from a remarkably high mortality rate, while their heirs – if traced at all – would inevitably be living abroad in obscure hideaways clearly devoid of any normal postal services. Interestingly, some of the larger publishing houses were often remarkably generous, even waiving the need for any payment at all. By contrast some of the smaller firms which might have been expected to be contented simply with a mention, were no way slow to exact their due pennyworths.

Meanwhile alongside this long-drawn-out costly exercise other wheels had been turning. Notably, John Birkbeck had put forward the inspired suggestion that an approach be made to SunPrint, the commercial print division of Scottish & Universal Newspapers, in Perth. It was a particularly happy move. What happened next was hard to believe. SunPrint's commercial print manager at that time, Bill Lockhart, at once took up the *Anthology* cause with the fervour of a personal crusade. His immediate first move was to approach the Jamieson and Munro Trust, a body ensuring that if printing work was scarce, SunPrint employees would be kept busy on the production of books of various kinds. The result was that it was agreed for the actual printing of the *Anthology* to be done free of cost to me apart from a nominal sum towards the production of the first print run.

The SunPrint relationship, fostered always so enthusiastically by Bill Lockhart, remained consistently happy for all of a dozen years, after which publishing changes had to be made. But above all I shall never forget that morning of 4 October 1988 when a SunPrint van arrived at our Aberfeldy front door and dropped its 50-box cargo of 500 copies of the *Anthology of Hope*. The 26-year dream had become reality after all. As I write now, stocks

An early nineties family group: Kenneth, Maisie and Campbell.

of the fourth printing of the *Anthology* are virtually at an end. All told, 3,500 copies have been produced.

Over the piece it has been my task to do the marketing, responding to orders from far and near, virtually keeping the postal service in business with a stream of weighty parcels. Not indeed the tale of a dozen years' hard toil, rather the components of a story that has been endlessly, without fail, rewarding.

While it has been the bigger booksellers such as Waterstone's and Wesley Owen (formerly Church of Scotland bookshops) who have, month after month, kept their stocks of the *Anthology* regularly topped up, very many smaller shops and Christian centres – for example the Abbey Bookshop on Iona – have played a wonderful part too.

So many kind friends have joined in over the years that it would be invidious to single out individuals. Suffice it to say that the help of many – some of whom have become voluntary 'agents' for their own area – has been immensely appreciated, while it has also been a privilege to strike up completely new and fascinating postal friendships.

Through the years too, it has been exciting to receive telephone calls and letters literally from all over the world: for example there was the surprise call from an unknown diplomat who told me he always carried an *Anthology* with him on his travels. One letter-writer stressed how grateful he was for the book's help in the running of his Bible study group in Guatemala. Nearer home there was the customer at an Edinburgh bookshop who confessed unashamedly to wanting a copy on the strength of having devoured a whole range of extracts by much squinting over the shoulder of a fellow passenger on the London train!

And yet, as the months and years have gone by, it has not been the humour, or the sales figures, the surprise requests from out of the blue, or even some of the remarkable answers to prayer in the 'dry' times, which have mattered most.

Rather it has been what can't be told: a story repeated time and time again; a story of ordinary folk, known and unknown, of friends or friends' friends, often of complete strangers, each for the most part questing for words of hope to pass on to some poor soul battered by personal grief.

All in all a story that from the start was meant to turn full circle.